THAI SOUP
A Thailand Dreamer Book

By

Milton David

New Generation Publishing

The Author wishes to convey special thanks, for their kind assistance with the writing of this story, to Jacqui Fogg and Martin Haley. He is grateful to both of them, for their advice about the content of his book.

Without them, it would not have been possible.

Milton David
August 2015

Note:

A 'farang' is a white person, male or female. It's more about skin colour than nationality. This expression comes from the Thai word for 'French' – (fanranzit)

The principal private hospital in Pattaya is called 'Bangkok Pattaya Hospital'

'Pick-up (truck)' This a van with covered but open back and 2 long seats. People stop the driver to say their destination, then go to the back to climb in. On arrival they ring the buzzer, get out and pay.

A Tuk-tuk is a small vehicle, taking up to 3 people only, which plies the streets of some parts of Thailand. As with the pickup truck, you stop it. State your destination and climb in at the side to sit on the long seat at the back. This is a 3 wheeler. The front looks like a motor scooter but it is totally covered by its roof and sides so that the passenger is 'in a cab' At the back, it has 2 wheels and the steering, at the front, is with one wheel.

INGREDIENTS

THAI SOUP

SILVER AND GOLD

In her village and those surrounding, people knew well the woman who called herself 'Madame Dee.' She had long straight hair like a young girl and a well-fleshed, and rather shapeless body. Her face showed all the lines and care of age. Madame Dee's eyes were penetrating. They seemed always to be looking at something that was much further than what was immediately before her. She wore a dark blue gown covered in astrological symbols.

Her daughter was home, which tended to change her to a less professional mode. It had been an enjoyable week for both of them and soon it would come to an end.

Vee sat her twenty-four year old body before her mother, with hope in her heart and the enthusiasm of youth. Her mother paused to consider how to convey some parting wisdom to her dear daughter, who to her, was always 'her little girl'. Eventually, she was ready. (Here is a translation)

"The Arabs have a saying, 'Words are of silver and Silence is golden.' They understand the difference. I will try to explain – You are to be between Silver and Gold," she finally announced. "Dear Mother, please tell me what this means."

"All right. Well, it's like this. Silver is the energy of movement, activity, curiosity, dynamism and change. This is the essential energy of the Earth's Element, Silver. Its partner, as we know is Gold – like Yin and Yang, Male and Female, Light and Dark. So we have Silver and Gold. The energy of gold is serenity, peace, tranquility, calmness and love. These two are the Earth's most valued elements."

"And I'm between the two – between rushing about and

1

chilling out?"

"Yeah, something like that, but you have to give each one a broad interpretation."

It was time to bid Mum farewell and take the bus back to Pattaya.

'I'm supposed to apply for that bank job', she told herself. 'I don't know about silver and gold – I think it's just the coins and banknotes of Thai money I'll be dealing with.'

So on Monday morning, she took the bus to Pattaya, as planned. From the bus station, she walked to the bank, carrying her casual clothes in a plastic bag. Vee had dressed smartly, in a white blouse and black skirt and top, as if she already was working there. But, they told her she lacked 'the experience they were looking for. – Well, may be working in a bank is not a job for me – surely it can be very dull sometimes,' she thought, as she changed clothes in the Ladies Room. She had the kind of figure that got in and out of jeans easily. She was soon done. She folded her 'business' clothes carefully and carried them in her plastic bag. In an effort to stay positive, she took a pick up to the sea front and decided to walk along the beach.

The first rays of sun made silver.

A slightly overweight bald-headed man walked along Pattaya beach, making for the restaurant, in the warming air.

"Hi Chicka, nice to meet ya," he said to the approaching girl.

"Sorry Sir, not my name," she said, drawing away from him as your pet dog might draw away from a tiger.

"Hey you," he began, grabbing her, "Your name is Chicka – I call you Chicka - geddit?"

"Chicka geddit," she repeated, realising she had no choice.

"Don't be funny," he said, giving her a shake. She glared at him.

2

"Your name is Chicka – Sit there!" he added, pointing at a chair.

He sat facing her.

"We drink and eat," he announced. 'Better to get something from him,' she allowed herself to think.

And silver danced on the waves.

He beckoned the waiter. There was some shouting between them which ended, "and don't be long about it!"

"Yes Sir! Ok Sir!" As the waiter rushed off, she wondered what he had ordered.

"Excuse me," she said, "I go toilet."

"How much," he barked, "How much to use toilet?"

"Don't know, may be 5/10 baht."

"There's two fives," he said, slapping two small coins on the table. She leaned forward to pick them up.

He grabbed her arm.

"Don't you be thinking of running off and not coming back, young lady – money you – purse / wallet, where?"

She took something from round her neck. "This purse me," she said. "Give it here!" he said. He released her arm, "Now go!"

She obeyed him and ran off towards the facilities building, still holding her plastic bag.

She used her solo time to try to think of some way of escaping from this horrible farang.

All she could think was, 'I get my purse back, then run for it –   Make for the Beach Road and jump on a pick-up truck.'

'Yeah, that's it! He wouldn't be that fast running after me.' She went through it, in her mind again, then returned to her table, fully resolved. But at this moment, the waiter appeared with a laden tray, and they went together to the table on the beach.

He was not there! What? Where was he? She and the waiter looked around. He placed his tray on the table. The chair had fallen over.

Ah! - There he was! Lying on his back, on the sand, with his eyes closed. The waiter righted the chair.

"Ok, I'll get an ambulance," she told the waiter, speaking in Thai. He took the tray of food back with him.

Her purse was lying next to the body. She repossessed it and phoned enquiries to get the number of Bangkok Pattaya Hospital, then called them for an ambulance. It took some explaining, in Thai, that the ambulance was not for her, but for a farang and he would pay. Hardly had she finished speaking, than a distant two-tone siren began. It gradually grew louder and louder. Two men with a stretcher rushed across the beach, and then returned with his body.

The ambulance set off, with its horns blasting again.

The sea was a steamy lake in a furnace.

....

Next day at 11 am, Vee went to Bangkok Pattaya Hospital, to ask about, "Farang - come in yesterday."

"Yes, Mr. Simmonds, in Ward 7, - What is your name? Vee showed her ID Card. "Visiting is from 10.45," she was told. She went to Ward 7 and was directed to the bed. Her contact details were taken.

"Miss Viraporn Willapana," the nurse announced.

"Oh, it's you – the last person I expected to see here."

"I called ambulance for you, Sir – are you better now?"

"Oh my God I had a heart attack. You saved my life!"

"Aray na? (What?) Sorry, no understand."

He leaned towards her. "You saved my life!" he said to her more emphatically, the tears running down his face

It was, in fact two days later, in the afternoon, when Rob Simmonds was allowed to leave hospital. Vee received a phone call from the hospital.

"I will take care him," she proudly announced, while hospital staff looked on, in stony-faced silence, as they had

4

heard these words, so many times before, from almost every girl-with-farang..

"My name Viraporn, but you can call me Vee," she explained.

"And my name's Rob," he replied.

"Well, Vee, I must apologise to you for my absolutely terrible behaviour. In fact, I have treated other girls badly, as well as you," he continued.

"You good, Rob, because you sorry and you not bad with woman like that again."

"It's kind of you to be so forgiving, Vee. The strange thing is, I need your help again. I have to go to the Immigration Police with my Passport, to get it stamped."

"No problem." Vee hailed a taxi and in just a few minutes they stopped at the Police Station. "Wait here please!" Rob said and went in. Vee stood in the street. After about 10 minutes, Rob emerged. "That's done!" was all he said. They both re-entered the taxi and he returned them to the beach area. Rob paid.

They discussed, what to do and where to go. Their agreed destination was the same beach table at the 'My Thai' restaurant-bar."

The waiter was delighted to see them.

They each had menus.

The sea was a glitter of gold.

ROB AND VEE -1

Rob discovered that Vee was a vegetarian. The waiter returned to ask if the food was ok. They both made compliments and thanked him.

"What I can't understand, Vee, is that after I had treated you so badly, you promptly phoned the hospital, and so, saved my life – I thought you would hate me and run off with your purse, leaving me, lying on the beach, to die there."

"I no can do that, Rob. I see man before, he lie on back – he eyes shut. He heart attack same like you."

"Really?"

"Yes, father me. We get with him to doctor as quick as possible, but him die."

"I am so sorry, Vee," Rob replied with watery eyes. Rob instinctively held her hand. "Why didn't you take him to the hospital?" he asked.

"We live in small village. Hospital many miles away in Pattaya or Bangkok. Also too much expensive for family me."

Rob took Vee back to his Hotel. In the back of the taxi they found each other's hands. Rob gave her a room in his suite. It was the first time she had been to the Royal Cliff Beach Hotel.

"Wow, you in this hotel?"

"Yes, that's right. You too!"

"But I not come here any time in my life!"

"Well, you are here now – all you have to do, is enjoy it!"

"Or, thank you, Mr. Rob."

They entered the suite and Rob showed Vee her room. She immediately went in with her luggage and started unpacking. Rob entertained himself by reading the Financial Times he had picked up downstairs, in the foyer. He was just starting an article about commodity trading when, suddenly, there was a knocking sound. He went to the connecting door of his suite and opened it. Vee stood looking at him.

"Hi, it's you!"

"Can I come speak to you?"

"Of course, you can. You are welcome. Come in. – Orange or pineapple juice?" he announced, opening the fridge.

"No thank you."

"Well what is it – what's on your mind?" he asked, holding her hands in his, and looking into her eyes.

"You like me, Rob?"

"Oh yes, of course I do,"

"Ok, me like you also."

They both then sat in armchairs and there was a table between them. Vee was the more upright of the two.

"Mr. Rob. You good man now. If you like me, so why leave me alone in another room?"

"My dear, I know very well what happens here in Thailand. A girl stays with a farang in his room – not to examine the wallpaper or watch TV."

"You mean, for sex."

"Yes, exactly. To me you are too special. I don't want to treat you, just as a girl for holiday sex, as many other farangs do."

"So you think me not attractive, like other girl. I don't have look in eye or I don't have good my body – may be too much fat. I not special."

"My dear - Please don't say you are not special. You are very attractive. I like your eyes and your body-shape – you are *not* fat at all!"

"So why I not with you?" she asked in exasperation.

"Ok. Come here and sleep in that bed!" he said, pointing to the other twin. She went back and forth from her room to his, bringing her personal luggage. She then sat down.

"So, no sex then?"

"That's right, my dear. You are too special, to me, for that right now."

7

"So may be later?"

"Yes, but 'later', does not mean later tonight or even next week. It may be a few months or may be a year."

"But then me older and you old man."

"Yes, you will be my old lady!" They both laughed. That night they both went to bed at 10.30pm.

....

Rob was awake early, as was his habit during his career as a Merchant Banker. Those days were over, but he still woke up. He sat reading his Financial Times quietly. He didn't need his glasses in the morning. He came across a 'Bangkok Post' newspaper and turned to the crossword.

Vee moved and just started to open her eyes.

"Good Morning my love, did you sleep well?"

"Yes, sleep very good – comfortable – bed sheet and pillow smell nice."

"Coffee?" Her face became a huge smile. Rob phoned room-service and ordered two coffees, then kissed her cheek. She immediately moved, thinking he was going to embrace her, but she just got up.

A knocking came to the door while Vee was in the bathroom. A tray was placed on the table. There was a milk jug, sugar and two steaming coffees. Rob handed the man a tip. He smiled and bowed politely as he left the room. Vee appeared in her underclothes, looking fully awake. She gathered her clothes and hurried back in to the bathroom. Rob waited patiently.

A little later, she appeared, fully dressed, with a towel on her head.

"Sorry, me slow."

Rob, still in his dressing gown, handed her a coffee. They both enjoyed their morning drink.

"Why didn't you use the dressing gown?" He asked, pointing to her one, still on its hook.

"Ok, next time," she replied, between sips. "I think you like to see me with only small clothes."

8

"Not important – one day I will see you with no clothes at all."

"Ok then, you want I have no clothes?"

"I would if I was an artist. I would paint a picture of you naked. But I am not an artist."

"What about you, Rob, you must have job something?" she asked becoming curious.

"Now I have no job. I retired – I stopped working early. I was a Merchant Banker. That's a banker who specializes in lending money to people who will pay back more."

"Wow, so you very rich?"

"Rich nit noy," (just a little) Rob replied, showing off his Thai. "I think," he began,

"Yes, my love? – ok I call you 'my love,' is it?"

"I think," Rob repeated,

"Yes, my love, that's ok, but I think we should go to see Lek today at the 'My Thai' restaurant-bar, but first we must have breakfast," he added.

"So now, you know same thinking me. I hungry."

SWIMMING

As soon as Rob had dressed, they went together down to the Hotel Restaurant, where there was a buffet-style breakfast lain out for guests.

After an enjoyable breakfast, they happened to walk past the swimming pool.

"Water nice," Vee observed, noticing the pool.

"You can swim?"

"No, sorry, no can swim."

"No problem, I teach you."

"Ok, thank you."

They were able to pick up a bikini type of costume for Vee at the general store in the foyer. They returned to the room, then emerged in their dressing gowns. There was just time for Vee to have her first swimming lesson.

They started in the shallow end. She splashed him and he splashed her.

"Let's swim!" Rob said.

"Cannot!"

"Ok, I teach you," he said taking her hands and starting to walk backwards. But she pulled herself towards him and clung to his body.

"Don't be afraid, even animals learn to swim."

"What?"

"Look - No, no animals here, only people – the water is clean and blue. It's beautiful – look!" She looked around and saw that Rob was right.

"Come on then, stretch your legs out and move them up and down, like this."

He showed her with his hands. They started again.

"That's right! Very good!" he said as they went across the width.

"Now, move your hands and arms like this. - Show me."

"That's right! Ok this time, when I let go of you, move your hands and arms like that and don't forget your legs - Ready?" He started to walk with her and then said,

10

"Ok, I'm going to let you go." He watched her struggling.

"Ok it's not easy but you are swimming!" She hugged him again and he hugged her.

"Now you are a swimmer!"

"Oh no!"

"Come on. Do it again. Show me your swimming." She set herself off and paddled away with her legs thrashing.

"Very good. You are a fantastic swimmer. You're a natural!"

They had to stop as Vee was becoming quite tired.

They put on their hotel robes.

"Next time, you'll be swimming same as me,"

Vee wasn't so sure.

As they returned to their room to shower and dress, she didn't answer.

Sitting alone in his room, Rob began to wonder if it was wise always to let Vee go first. Eventually, his turn came.

So it was around midday, that they went, yet again, to their customary table on the Public Beach – the 'My Thai' restaurant-bar.

Their friendly waiter was there as usual, but he looked sad and worried about something.

"Hey, I don't even know your name," Rob began.

"I am Lek – Lek Charoenkul - I *was* a waiter. But the boss has just fired me from next month. He says he wants to sell up and go. So from next month I am nothing and nowhere. I am worried because my family."

"We are sorry you problem," Vee said for both of them. Rob said nothing.

"Well, can I take your order?" he asked, suddenly reviving.

They both chose from the menu and Lek went off to the kitchen.

"What about you, my special one – what do you do for

11

a job?"

"Well I can do accounting so I tried a bank job, but they say me no have experience." (she paused)

"Excuse me Rob," she began again, "Why you say 'special one'?"

"Because that's what you are to me – my 'special one'."

Vee could not stop herself smiling.

"I'm glad you are happy about that."

A moment later, Lek arrived with a tray full of food.

"Hey, Lek!"

"Yes Sir! What can I do for you?" he asked, as he served out the food.

"May I have your mobile number?"

"Yes Sir, just a minute." He searched through his shirt pocket for a piece of paper. A moment later a paper with Lek's name and number was in Rob's hand.

"Thank you Lek! - I wish you good luck."

"Thank you, Sir, you are very kind. Please enjoy your food"

BAN NONG CHIM - 1 and ENGLISH

Later, sitting in the foyer of the Royal Cliff beach Hotel, Vee could see that Rob had something on his mind. Rob, you very thinking – why you not tell me?"

"Ok, we must do something about your English – that's why you can't get a job!"

"Oh – English me very bad?"

"Nothing about you is very bad but your English is, as you would say, 'very no good.'"

"Oh, so sorry. I try to make better."

"Well, what do you think about going to a School to study English and learn to speak just like me?"

"Good idea, Rob, but expensive."

"Don't worry about what it costs. I will pay for everything. I think the best School is called 'The British Council,' they are in Bangkok, Siam Square."

"But this Pattaya - very big travelling!"

"True, but I think, may be better to do some different big travelling first," Rob replied.

"What you mean? I not understand."

"Well, I expect you would like to see your family, wouldn't you?"

"Oh yes very much, can we visit them, Rob?"

"Certainly, but do you mind if I come along with you?"

"No, my love, I not mind. I want you come with me. I want family me meeting you, okay?"

"Yes, that's good, thank you for your invitation! It'll be great!"

"Journey from here, not very great - two buses and one pick-up truck."

"Better I think one taxi, isn't it?" Rob replied.

"Or! - you will take taxi from Pattaya to Ban Nong Chim? - I will be arriving like   Rajdamree."

"That's quite right, because you are a Princess!"

It was evening, when their taxi reached the village of Ban Nong Chim.

There was an unmade road. Grass and various trees grew all around the houses. Many were little more than piles of seasoned wood, to look at. Here and there, stood a more conventional house, showing the glass, browns and metalwork of modern building materials. There were people and dogs around and everywhere was hot.

"I go talk to my mother first. Then I come to you. Wait here with bags, please." Vee went to one of the smarter looking houses.

It was the garden of this house, at the far side, which had the cesspit cover that the lorry called at to empty. Like her neighbours, Vee's house had a huge tank-like pot, at the back of the house, that was used to collect rain water. Also a tank in the roof was filled from time to time. The local shop sold electric fans and bottled water. So it was survivable, for anyone who happened to be in good health.

....

Rob, having dismissed the taxi, stood guard over the bags. Children appeared and stared at him.

"Hallo Sir, How are you?" said one who giggled and ran away. Vee reappeared.

"Mother me has security problem. She much money and jewellery but can put in cupboard with padlock. Not good because may be, kamoy (thief) come. She want go Bangkok, to do Bank deposit."

"Well, she's welcome to come with us when we go," Rob said.

"Ok, we tell her." Rob picked up the bags. Vee helped him and they went into the house. Vee introduced her mother. Rob smiled and bowed politely. They sat round a table. There were glasses of water. Rob asked Vee,

"Is there a restaurant anywhere near here."

"Yes in Prachin Buri. It's about 15 minutes on the pick-up truck – I think good idea we go there, ok with you, Rob?"

"Sure, great idea!"

14

"Ok I tell my mother to be ready." Rob, and Vee's mother stood outside the house. Vee went off to get the pick-up truck. When she returned with the transport, they went to the restaurant in Prachin Buri and the truck waited for them.

Vee explained to Rob, that a number of her mother's clients had given her extra presents as well as her fee, hence the jewellery and valuables she had amassed. A lad from Dubai had come, only last week and she had given him advice as usual. He had paid twice her fee and gone away but, now he emailed her to say she was absolutely right and he had been very successful. He had started telling his friends that this 'amazing Lady in Thailand', was able to tell the future accurately.

"It looks like my mum's business is doing very well," Vee remarked to him. The food was not amazing but quite good. Rob and Vee gave it 5 out of 10.

Vee's mum, seemed to enjoy it. When they returned, Vee showed Rob where they would sleep - and the bathroom. Soon, they were both sleeping soundly, after an exhausting day. It was Rob's first experience of rural life in Thailand.

Next day, Rob met Vee's two teenage brothers, Tarrin and Jira, who did odd jobs around the village, to make themselves a living. He was surprised to find that they could speak English and obviously had some education. Tarrin asked Rob how difficult it was, for Thai people, to get a visa to enter the UK. Rob explained as truthfully, but briefly, as he could. Jira said he wanted to start a business, but he wasn't sure how he could do it. Both lads looked scruffy and as if they had been just called away from some sort of major cleaning job, but they were willing to listen politely to the farang. Rob took their mobile numbers.

Vee announced that she and her mum were ready. Vee then went off to get the taxi. Minutes later, it arrived. Mother sat in front, with the driver. Rob and Vee shared the back seat.

"We go first to Bangkok Bank, in Silom Road," Rob announced to the driver, "then take us to Siam Square - You then come back to the Bank, here, to collect Mother of Vee and take her back to Ban Nong Chim."

Vee translated for the driver and then explained to her mother that she would be taken back in the taxi and we would remain in Bangkok.

....

Rob found an apartment. It was by no means luxurious but it was clean and the people were friendly. They asked for twin beds and were told -

"No problem!" They put their things down and Rob said,

"Let's go to the British Council now – I think they are still open."

"Yes, ok. But they very expensive, Rob"

"You let me worry about that my dear."

"Oh thank you Rob, you very good man now."

They locked up, taking their key and it was literally, just round the corner.

"They will probably give you a test to check which class to put you in," Rob announced to her. They entered the British Council Building.

"Hello, new student?"

"Yes please," Rob said. A young man took Vee aside and spoke with her for a few minutes. He then checked her in to the beginners' class. Rob booked her for the whole course. They were given a brochure. The teacher's name was 'Kayleigh.'

"Hungry?" Rob asked.

"What about this place?"

"No wait, I show you good Thai place." Vee walked fast and Rob followed. They turned a corner and she walked on. Suddenly she said,

"Here!" It was very crowded but some people got up to

16

go, so they just managed to get a table. A waiter came and cleared the table. Then he wiped it clean and set it out ready for them. The Menu was all in Thai. Vee did her best to translate.

"I like hot, but only a little bit," Rob explained.

"You like coconut?"

"Yes, I do, very much."

"What about chicken or fish?"

"No I want to be vegetarian like you."

"Ok, I order – you and me together."

Vee called the waiter and placed the orders.

"To drink we have orange, pineapple or mango juice," the waiter said in English. Vee asked for pineapple and Rob ordered mango.

So together they had a pleasant evening celebrating their day's successful business.

"Don't forget – lessons start at 9.30 am tomorrow," in Room 12 upstairs, it says here," Rob, read from the brochure.

BUSINESS - 1

While Vee was at her classes, Rob kept himself busy. First, he had to check with the Police Station. He knew Vee would be away until 4.30 in the afternoon, so he called at the Immigration Police Station and got the new date stamp for his passport. He then returned to Sukhumvit Road and sat in a coffee shop making a business plan – at least, putting together the necessary ideas, to give birth to his business. He was thinking of involving Lek, Tarrin and Jira, if he could create a going concern. He and Vee would have to get it started. Rob made a note of all his deliberations, so that he had the rudiments of a plan. He then went to the Naraya Phand shop in the new 'Hotel International' and selected from the brooches, an orchid set in gold. It was neatly placed, in a small box and in a bag, which Rob put in his briefcase. 'This is for when she can have a proper conversation with me,' Rob told himself. He made his way slowly back to Siam Square, using the sky walk. Rob stopped to look at Erewan Shrine, where there was music and Thai Classical Dancing. He then continued along the corridor above the pollution and bustle of the street below. The huge Paragon shopping mall loomed up on his left and just after this, he was at Siam Station.

It was time to descend to street level and find Siam Square. He arrived at The British Council, and there, standing outside, Vee was waiting for him. They hugged and he kissed her cheeks.

"I'm hungry!" he suddenly said.

"Me too!"

"Same place as before?"

"Yes ok, good."

"How was the English lesson?" Rob asked as they were striding towards the restaurant.

"Ok. We learn Hello, How are you? My name is Vee, and you?"

"Wow, all that - that's fantastic!"

They entered the restaurant. They ordered, as before and Rob decided to give Vee just some idea about his plan.

....

Life went on for several weeks, in this manner. Rob found a better looking restaurant to take Vee to. One day, when he met her, he just said,

"This time, you follow me." They took the sky train to Nana and walked to the entrance of the Landmark Hotel.

"Or! - this must be very expensive!" she said to Rob.

"More than that place in Siam Square but it's much more comfortable and I think the food is better," Rob added. They went to the coffee shop.

"Sorry, it's mostly farang food here," Rob said.

"Mai pen rai, It's ok," Vee replied, suddenly realizing she had spoken Thai. Rob ordered Mushroom Quiche and Vee found something Thai. When Vee's came, Rob said,

"That looks very healthy! Can I try some?"

"Be careful, it's hot – a lot chilli," she said, pushing her plate to him. Rob took some of the greenery.

"This name 'som-tam.' – Can I try some of yours?"

She cut a small piece.

"Wow, it really nice. I have this next time." Rob and Vee both ate enthusiastically. They then had coffees.

The following day, the order was

"Two mushroom quiches please,"

"Is that name for it – 'musloom kish?'"

"Not quite," Rob said. "It's like the word 'tea' – 'quiche', Rob repeated. Vee laboured with it, but she couldn't get it.

Then, Rob realised this would be a job for the school.

"Mai pen rai," he said to Vee.

"Or! you speak Thai!" She was surprised that he could say something in Thai.

The quiches came and they both ate with gusto.

So they went several times to the coffee shop of the Landmark, for the unpronounceable farang food.

After about a month, Vee announced that she was now

in the intermediate class. Rob was pleased that she had been promoted so fast. "Intermediate-1" she explained.

"Also, do you mind if we don't have quiche, but something Thai?"

"That's ok," Rob replied. Rob went with her to the Thai restaurant in the Landmark Hotel. Many dishes were put on the table and they both enjoyed the food.

"I want you to know that my mum now has good business, from Arabs in Middle East. They pay her big money and tell their friends. My mum, she want sell her house and come to Bangkok with lorry, for new house. I think she will go to Bang Na. I tell you this, because she give me money, so sometime I pay – not always you Rob. I know you very kind, but I also know about money."

"That's kind of you to offer. It's not that I don't want your money. Couldn't we use it later?"

"You mean, to buy a restaurant bar?"

"Yes, for something like that." Rob said, not sure what would be needed or when.

"Meanwhile – while we are waiting, you put this money in your bank account – ok?"

"Sure. Good idea." They finished their meal with a popular Thai dessert, 'Lot Tong.'

Their life in Bangkok continued. Vee studied. They enjoyed each other's company.

Eventually Vee announced she was in Intermediate-3

"Still not Advanced?" was Rob's comment.

"Advanced English is needed for University level – Oh, and by the way, there is also Intermediate 4."

"I think you had better do that too."

…………………………..

So, as before, their Bangkok life continued. They were both waiting for something.

Months went by and the day came when Vee met Rob with a large envelope.

"My Certificates," she explained.

20

Rob took her to the largest restaurant in the world, Tam Nak Thai, down by the river. The waiters went about their business on roller skates. Food was ordered and arrived quite promptly.

"I want to tell you something Rob. In the British Council a nice farang boy started to talk with me. He wanted to make a date. I lied to him. I just said,

"Sorry, I'm married." I cannot put anyone else before *you*, Rob. You are my man here in Thailand. What I cannot understand is you don't come to me to make love. May be I am not good enough for you. I know I am not very good-looking. So you don't love me...."

"Wait a .minute!" Rob interrupted, "Please don't say that, I know you are beautiful. But beauty within is more important than beauty of the face and body."

"So I still don't understand why you treat me just like a friend but not like a lover."

"That's because, my dear Vee, I am much older than you. I could even be your father. Make no mistake, I love you very much. To me, no other woman in Thailand (or anywhere else!) is more important, than you. You can be a good business partner. But I cannot make love with you. Many farangs come to Thailand and make love with any girl they meet. But you are not 'any girl' you are special. I respect you too much to treat you as cheaply as other farangs treat their girls."

"Ok. I understand. I respect you too, Rob," there were tears in her eyes.

"If you should have any doubt about my feelings for you – I would like you to have this little present," Rob produced a small bag from his brief case.

Vee wondered what on earth it could be. She removed the box – opened it – and gasped,

"Oh, this is lovely. Gold and ruby – it must have been very expensive," she said to Rob.

"Yes, my love, I thought it was right for you. Vee kissed his cheek.

....

That evening, back in the apartment, Rob looked at Vee's certificates. He selected the most recent one,

"Intermediate – 3" and said to her,

"We can get this one framed. Eventually, it will go up on the wall of our restaurant."

"So every farang will expect to chat with me."

"Not every farang, but some will, – it will help us to attract good customers. When does your Intermediate 4 finish?"

"In two weeks, I think."

Rob and Vee continued for a further two weeks. Rob taking her to various restaurants of his choice, each afternoon, after school. Their conversation flourished. He noticed that her English was gradually improving.

The day arrived when Vee met him with another brown envelope.

"My new Certificate!" Rob took it out and examined it.

"So, Intermediate - 4 now?"

"Yes, that's right."

"Another frame, I think."

"Ok, thank you. Isn't it time to contact Lek?" Vee asked.

"Oh yes, thank you, I forgot - ok, you phone and speak Thai, then translate for me," he said, taking out his piece of paper with Lek's phone number.

"Ok."

"Halo, Khun Lek, chai mai ka?" (Is that Lek?)

"Ok, what do you want me to say to him?"

"I want him to be my partner in business." Vee translated.

"Yes, very interested but what kind of business? Lek asked."

"We run a restaurant together." She told Lek.

"But he has very little money, same his brother. Tan and his other brother, who was cook at Mai Thai, name, Prem, the same," he said.

Vee explained.

"No, problem, they can learn the job like you. You and

Prem will show Tan what to do and how to do it." Vee translated again.

"Where will this restaurant be?"

"Don't know yet, probably Pattaya. I want us all to meet in Pattaya this coming week.. Let's say Wednesday 10 am at 'Indian by Nature' on Thappraya Road. We can sit in the lobby-bar and talk." Vee translated.

"He will check with the others and phone you this evening." Vee said.

"Now we must meet your two brothers and go to Pattaya with them."

"We can meet them on Tuesday." Vee replied.

"Good thinking, partner, but we can go now, can't we?"

"Yes, I was getting tired of Bangkok," she replied.

....

They seemed to have accumulated more luggage from somewhere. Rob collected everything from the apartment he had rented.

It all went into a couple of travel bags in the boot of the taxi. They arrived at the Royal Cliff Beach Hotel.

"We go to Ban Nong Chim tomorrow. Today is Swimming Day!" Rob announced.

"Oh no it's not. Sorry, Rob. I cannot swim today because it's my period."

"Oh sorry, darling, I just didn't think. I just opened my mouth and the words came out."

"Mai pen rai," they both said together, then laughed.

Sitting under a sunshade on the hotel's private beach, they were both in the mood for a lazy afternoon.

"Coconut is very good for you," she said, seeing that they were coming round. Rob bought two and handed Vee one. They rested again, sucking straws – the sea gently lapping and kids running about. Rob saw what Vee did with the metal spoon and copied her. Vee went off to the bathroom, and Rob continued his semi-consciousness. Vee returned. Rob was looking about him wondering where she had gone.

"I brought you a menu!" Vee said chirpily.

"Good, I was starting to feel hungry," His phone rang. He handed it to Vee.

"Lek," he said. They talked. She finished the call.

"It's ok Rob, they can all come."

"Well, now it seems you have to learn French," Rob said, glancing at the menu.

'Bouef en Croute, how pretentious,' Rob thought to himself. They both chose a vegetarian option.

They asked for juice to drink.

"How are you feeling now?"

"Nice of you to think of me, I am ok, thank you, not wonderful, but ok."

"Excuse me, Vee, but you are especially wonderful today." She laughs.

"Not sick?"

"No, very wonderful, not sick!"

"I ask you only because most Thai girls – er well, never mind."

"Exactly, mai pen rai. – You funny!" Vee said, quite forgetting she was Intermediate 4 English.

They smiled at each other.

"May be you are more like my dad," Rob didn't answer.

"At one time I had an English wife," he began. We never had any children but I always thought I could have been a good dad."

"She alive now?"

"No, she got a Cancer problem. It got worse and she died." I just went on working and saving my money, so that I could come to Thailand. Many friends had told me it was wonderful.

One girl I got to know, stayed with me. Then one day, I came out of the bathroom quicker that she expected and I caught her with *her* hand in my wallet. She went and the next girl stole my bag. I had a call from the bus station, to go and pick it up. She had taken my passport, my camera and the UK cash I had in one of the pockets. I made up my mind that Thai girls were out to get what they want from *me* – so *I* would get what I want from *them*. I think you know the rest of this story, because you were on the receiving end."

"Yes, I remember- 'your name chicka, geddit'?"

"Ok but I never, in my dreams, imagined I would find a Thai girl like you, my darling Vee. If No Vee, then no Rob. I am here happy and alive today only BECAUSE YOU ARE A GOOD GIRL!" Rob said in his paternal way.

Vee immediately embraced and kissed his cheek. It was soon evening. Rob booked a taxi for the next morning. They went to their room. They had a much better understanding now, than the first time they came here. Showers, bed and sleep.

....

Tuesday morning came. They were both up bright and early. Rob and Vee took themselves to breakfast. It was a buffet. They each selected, and with laden plates, went to a table. There was water on the table.

"Shall I get some coffees?"

"Yes please, my love," she replied. He returned, holding a small tray, with two coffees, sugar and milk. Rob drank his coffee and relaxed. It also helped to wake him up at this hour of the morning. Vee enjoyed it too.

"What's that stuff, Rob?"

"It's called, Meusli," he replied, moving it towards her.

"Try it?"

"Ok" She took her spoon.

"Oh sweet and milky."

"You try this?"

"What is it?"

"Rice soup," She pushed it towards him. Rob tried it.

"Ok, but wow it's hot!"

"Yes, it has chilli but you can ask them to put less chilli in it."

They returned to their own breakfasts.

"Excuse me Sir, your Taxi for Ban Nong Chim, is here."

"Thank you, please tell him to wait 15 minutes."

"Yes Sir." As soon as they had finished their food, they returned to the room. Rob checked his briefcase. They took their clothes, bathroom bits and quickly put all their luggage in Rob's bag. A final check and look around. Rob found a lipstick in the bathroom.

"This is yours?"

"Oh thanks, I forgot it!" She put it in her handbag. There was a knock at the door.

"Come in please," Rob said. A man took the luggage down to the waiting taxi. Vee with her handbag and Rob with his briefcase then followed. Rob slipped the man some money. He smiled and bowed. They sat together in the back. The journey began.

BAN NONG CHIM -2

They both took an opportunity to shut their eyes again. There was the comfort of soft upholstery and gentle air conditioning. Very Soon they were both dozing. As they leaned towards each other, they gave and received support. The driver noticed this in his mirror and drove at an easy pace. As they went through Chachoensao, Vee woke up. She sat straight and Rob, being heavier than her, then flopped on to her lap and began to snore. It took all the driver's self-control, not to burst out laughing, at what he saw in his mirror. Vee glared at him, unamused. Suddenly, the taxi braked hard and jerked to a stop, as an ox-drawn cart rumbled across the road in front of them. Rob shuddered and woke, surprised and embarrassed to find himself on Vee's lap.

"Oh, I'm so sorry,"

"Don't worry. Did you have a nice sleep?"

"Yes, thank you, my love, thanks to you, again, for looking after me."

"But that's my job and it's the best job I've ever had in my life."

"That's very sweet of you, but I want you to have a better job."

Vee didn't answer. The taxi was now starting to gather speed again.

....

'CUTIE'

Their destination, was a village where there were a lot of girls, several SooSoo's age. – Her real name was 'Sasithorn', but like most Thais, she always used her nickname. (She had taken more care in composing it, than others take.) It seemed, to SooSoo, that all the girls became teenagers together. According to her, the only interesting thing to do in Ban Nong Chim, was to give looks to boys and see their reaction. In most cases they would drool over her and the bolder ones would try to start a conversation. SooSoo had been blessed with a healthy body and the sort of face and eyes that were a good advertisement for 'anything'- she supposed. She had no trouble keeping boys in tow and the other girls tried, desperately, to emulate her.

All this was little more than innocent childish fun, until, one of her friend's uncles, 'Chimi', took a shine to her. He had a permanent smile, or was it a leer? Anyway, SooSoo didn't like him. She couldn't say what it was, but there was something about him that made her afraid.

Then, one Saturday afternoon, she will never forget, he became nice and friendly. SooSoo's father had died several years ago and this man seemed to talk as *he* would have done. His kind and easy words filled her with a sense of comfort and excitement. She remembers in detail, how she was persuaded, to eagerly follow him to his room. 'This man is just fun! He could keep me interested and feeling good all the time!' she felt, as she blindly strode to keep up with him.

The outcome of this, her biggest adventure in life, so far, was, that she lost her virginity. She had allowed herself to be taken in by this horrible man. The price she had paid was to have her youth stolen from her. It was not the pain and having to hobble home, but a feeling of shame and loss that overwhelmed her. 'You will never be innocent again' the voice in her head said. She felt both unclean and foolish. For the first time in her life, her self-esteem was at a very low ebb. Meeting her mother, brought an angry crying outburst, from both of them – accusations in anger and bitterness.

……………………………

As soon as she had recovered, SooSoo did her best to keep up her image with the other girls. It came to her a surprise, when Jira Willapana showed an interest in her. No longer being able to give him the same flashes and runabout, she had given to other boys, she became suddenly self-conscious, which made her angry.

"So, why are you talking to me? You know who I am. I usually take 5 minutes with boys like you." Jira stood fast and waited.

"I don't think there's any hurry, is there?"

"Why you come and talk to me?"

"I am like all other boys. I see you flash your eyes and I can't resist you."

"Ha ha, just what I thought!"

"I thought you'd be pleased. You are exceptionally attractive, you know." SooSoo, for the first time in her life, didn't know what to say. Then, it came to her.

"Maybe I am, as you say, but what you don't know, is that I have a dirty little secret."

"Well, *I* 've been with other girls," Jira admitted.

"Yes, that's normal – but now, I feel dirty."

"I don't know what you mean."

SooSoo then told Jira the story of how she lost her virginity. As she finished, she was close to tears. Jira embraced her and held her.

"We all make mistakes," he murmured. – None of this was known to Rob and Vee –

SooSoo invited Jira home, to meet 'Mum'

This time the meeting was successful.

Rob and Vee's taxi arrived at Ban Nong Chim.

They stopped at the house.

"Please tell, Tarrin and Jira, to be ready in about 30 minutes, to come with us. Tell them it's to attend a meeting tomorrow in Pattaya about a business opportunity."

"Ok, but I see my mum first,"

Rob waited patiently,

"Ok if I sleep in your taxi?" he asked the driver.

"No problem, Sir. Me and you same – sleep maak maak (a lot)," he explained with a big smile on his face. So these two men began to doze.

Boisterous conversation in Thai, woke both of them. Vee, in jeans and tee-shirt and carrying no more than her handbag, in which she had put one of her framed certificates, to show her mother, suddenly appeared. Then came Tarrin and Jira, hauling large bags. They were hardly recognisable from before. They both had haircuts which made a great improvement to their appearance. Their clothes were clean and smart-looking too. Obviously, they had made a conscientious effort to look their best, and Jira had a dazzling piece of womanhood on his arm. She was, 'SooSoo,' the cutie of Ban Nong Chim! Apparently, he took her seriously! Vee deliberately ignored SooSoo. She was sad and angry, that her brother had chosen this girl, who was 'nothing but a slut,' in Vee's estimation. Jira was in the process of bidding her farewell.

"My mum wants to come too, is that ok?" (She still ignored SooSoo.)

"All right," Rob said. Vee called out to her. The driver added Madame Dee's rather bulky bag, to the boot.

So four squeezed themselves into the back. SooSoo wandered off, gradually leaving Jira's gaze.

PATTAYA

Vee had second thoughts and went to the front to sit on Rob's lap.

"Di qua, mai?" she asked (Is that better?) Vee's mum with her two boys, in the back, were well-pleased with their new-found comfort. The taxi moved off. Both Rob and Vee enjoyed their first experience of physical closeness to each other. He could sense her whole body – its womanly smell and pulses.

She, in turn was impressed by the gentle muscles of his arms and surprisingly soft hands. The conversation in the back was all in subdued Thai.

Rob told the driver to go to the Royal Cliff Beach Hotel in Pattaya. He got them all checked in and said,

"We stay here tonight and leave here at 9.30 am tomorrow to go to our business meeting. We dine in one hour – That's 7.00pm in the restaurant over there, Rob said, pointing." Vee translated.

Everyone went excitedly to the room on their key tag, as porters carried their luggage. Rob and Vee went together to see that Vee's mum was ok. She found her room. Rob and Vee, like everyone else did their bathroom things, got changed and made sure they were quite ready for the two grand social occasions before them.

The two boys plus Rob and Vee arrived almost together. The boys had black trousers and white shirts. Rob had a dark grey suit and the striped tie from his old school. Vee wore a dark blue sari which went perfectly with her long dark hair. They arrived in the Dining area and were choosing an aperitif as Vee's mum, 'Madame Dee' arrived hiding her rather large figure in a sumptuous leaf- green sari. Taking their drinks they got seated and began the serious business of consulting menus.

For Rob and Vee, it was a simple matter of choosing a vegetarian dish. Rob insisted that everyone should have anything they liked and suggested –

"Think about putting dishes in the middle for everyone to share. Vee and I are vegetarian." Vee translated this.

The dishes arrived. Madame Dee also had vegetarian food, Tarrin had fish and Jira had

"Bof en Crot – what is this?" he asked, pointing at the menu.

"Boef en Croute, Sir. It's French. It means Beef wrapped in pastry, would you like to try it?"

"Yes please."

There were dishes of mixed vegetables. Carrots and peas with the fish. The vegetarians had a brown rice and vegetables. There was also a selection of patties made with seeds and lentils. There was Soy Sauce on the table.

A small jug came.

"This is gravy, it is a type of sauce, made with juices from the meat, to go on the boeuf en croute and with your vegetables," the waiter explained to Jira. Much enthusiastic eating followed. Rob asked for a non-alcoholic Sangria and glasses. There was also a jug of water. This was the grandest feast these boys had ever had in their lives.

The waiter returned with the dessert menus. There was mango and sticky rice, 'Tutti-Fruiti' ice-cream or sherry trifle.

"Tutti-fruiti means, with many different kinds of fruit." The waiter explained. Coffee was also on offer. Rob and Vee got the ice-cream *and* sherry trifle, to share with each other. Tarrin had mango and sticky rice and when Jira saw it he ordered the same as his brother. Madame Dee just had a coffee. Vee spent much of her time, hard at work, translating. They all knew that Rob wanted them to be partners and tomorrow they would meet three new (probable) partners. Rob was thanked by everyone and they retired to their rooms.

"Thank you Rob for giving my mum and my brothers such a nice meal. It was very kind of you."

"You ain't seen nothing yet," Rob replied.

"Aray, na?" (What?)

32

"I mean it's only a little thing. The big thing will be tomorrow when we and those three lads, join us for lunch, together at "'Indian by Nature'" - the restaurant up the hill, on Thappraya Road.

"Ok I understand. I hope this works successfully for you Rob." They continued their chatter for a while as they were getting ready for bed. Then it was lights out.

BUSINESS MEETING -1

The big day arrived. Behind the closed doors of a certain guest corridor there was a flurry of activity as certain guests showered – put bathrooms to full use and consulted mirrors. Two doors opened and four smart-looking people marched towards the lift. Somebody called something in Thai. They waited with open doors and Vee's mother arrived, in a purple sari.

In Rob's outfit, only his tie was the same as yesterday. His suit was dark blue. Vee had a bright orange sari to offset her long dark hair. The lads were smart. The lift descended – opened and five guests set out with plates to sample the breakfast buffet. They ate quietly and drank their coffee. "We are in good time – so take it easy," Rob announced. "We'll all meet again here when we are ready."

There was a return to rooms and bags, rucksacks, brief cases and folders were prepared – pens placed in pockets. There was a final look in mirrors before zero hour. Rob and Vee down in the lobby were soon joined by the others. Rob asked the desk for a Limousine. Almost instantly it arrived and doors were opened. This time all four could get comfortably into the back and Rob sat in front with the driver.

"Just ''Indian by Nature',' Sir?" he enquired.

"Yes please. That's right," Rob replied, as the car swooped off with a huff. In just minutes they were cruising to a halt outside the restaurant.

"Good Morning – Mr. Simmonds?" a uniformed doorman enquired.

"Yes please," Vee responded, as Rob was tipping the Limousine driver and collecting together his guests.

They entered and looked in amazement at the exotic décor. It is was if a piece of the jungle from India had been recreated in this cool corner of Thailand. They were shown in to a conference room. A jug of water and glasses were placed on the table. Rob began,

"I would like to thank you all for coming. Where is Vee?" he suddenly asked in some alarm.

The door opened again and Vee entered, followed by two casually dressed figures, a thick-set short and rather surly young man, a second young man who was tall, wiry and energetic. They were followed by Lek. Vee introduced Prem and Tan to the group. The tall smartly dressed and ever-smiling, Lek, was of course, already well-known and smart as usual.

"Excellent. Thank you my dear," Rob said, realising he had forgotten about them. Rob started again.

"I'd like to thank you all for coming here today to discuss our business venture. We are going to open a restaurant cafe here in Pattaya. I just want to outline what I would like each one of you to do." Vee translated.

"First, I would like to introduce you all to Prem and Lek. They will be your teachers – Everyone here will have two jobs – it's called OJT 'on the job training' - you learn the job while you're doing it. – Prem is an experienced Chef and Lek is an experienced waiter. So one of them will be teaching you the job." Vee again translated.

Vee suddenly asked,

"but what am I going to do?" which caused some amusement.

"You will be my trainee manager," he replied. Vee didn't translate.

Her mother said, "Or! Vee deejan, kao ja poojatkhan!" (Oh, my Vee is going to be a manager!)

"Does that mean we work for a woman?" Lek asked.

"Most of the time, yes, - but first, Miss Vee will learn from me, how to manage the business. If you should prefer to bring a problem directly to me – that's up to you. –

The Restaurant-bar will be called, "'Rob and Vee's'"

Tan spoke to Vee in Thai.

"He wants to know if he can be a chef, like his brother, Prem." she said.

"Certainly," tell him, "but I don't want anyone to rush into a decision. Think it over for the next 2 weeks and then

35

let one of us know. This is important for everybody here."

At this point Vee and her mum went into a huddle.

"My mother says she can help you find a property to buy."

"Thank you," Rob replied smiling and nodding to her.

"Ok so we are all partners. We will all be paid a percentage of the profits." Vee translated.

"Are you all with us?" Rob asked. Vee, again translated. There was general acceptance and Rob and Vee went round the table shaking hands with everyone.

"Hieoo Kao" (I'm hungry) said Madame Dee. Vee whispered to Rob. They all stood and filed out to the restaurant. As they left Rob passed each one, a piece of paper with his and Vee's phone numbers.

Madame Dee, looking resplendent in her purple Sari, said something in Thai.

"Indian food is her favourite," Vee said.

....

They all enjoyed a thoroughly delicious meal, dipping from time to time into the array of dishes set out before them.

"This is to celebrate the start of our business. I need you and you need me, if we are to be successful" Rob said. Vee translated.

"Before you leave today, please make sure either I, or Vee, have your mobile number and email address, if you have one." Vee responded, briefly, again. But everyone was far too busy eating, to say anything.

To follow, came an assortment of Indian sweets – Ledou, Ice Halwa, Gajjar ka Halwa, Barfi, Rasmalai, Gulab Jamon, Jalebis and Kulfi (Indian Ice-cream). There was a general feeling that if coffees were not ordered they would never be able to get up again.

So ended a delightful meal and everyone thanked Rob for his kindness and generosity. Vee smiled and felt very proud of him.

Suddenly Madame Dee had something to say. She spoke to her daughter in Thai.

"My mother says she has seen the property you need and she wants to buy it for you. So she will be a 'sleeping partner,' I think you say?"

"Quite correct my dear but what property, where?"

"After this, when we have had a chance to recover, she will take us to have a look."

"Ok, you had better tell everyone that we will meet again same place, same time in two weeks' time – but only to talk. No more food, I promise, you won't be hungry by then." Vee translated. Good-byes were said and thanks again.

"Don't forget 2 weeks from now –" Rob said with Vee's help. The four young men went off, chatting together eagerly.

PROPERTY CHECKS

Rob and Vee, then placed themselves in the hands of Madame Dee. The taxi went down the hill and turned right into 'third road', then along to Pattaya Klang, turned left, then left again, into Soi Burkao, went along, then, in order to get the opposite one-way system, turned right between buildings, back alleyways and the odd bar here and there, until it reached the back of a shop. Going round it, they turned right into Second road and the taxi pulled up. Madame Dee paid the driver. Rob and Vee were mystified.

They went in and ordered drinks. Seven up, Fanta and Madame Dee had Spry. This gave them a chance to look around. They seemed to do mostly Indian food. There was only one waiter. Only one person sat there eating – A youth in a vest and shorts who had a kebab with his beer.

When the waiter came with the tab, Vee asked in Thai, "Who is the boss man here, can you give me name and phone number?" The answer in Thai, was,

"Why? - you want to complain about something"

"No, we want to buy this place."

"Or ok!" was the enthusiastic response. A Thai man emerged from the back of the shop.

"This Boss man," the waiter said in English.

"Can we look round this building, do you mind?" Vee asked in Thai. The 3 followed him into the kitchen. Clearly it needed a good clean-up, but it seemed to be well-equipped. Back in the shop area there were some tables and chairs. He explained in Thai that he had more tables and chairs in a store room. They noticed some land at the back with long grass, and were told that it belonged to the shop.

"Can we see somewhere else?" Rob asked. Vee translated. Madame Dee said something. "Yes she will show us two more," Vee explained, as they left.

"This place is low on ambience. I mean, all you can look at is passing traffic and the interior of the shop has only bare walls, no windows or alcoves," Vee translated. Her mother spoke again and Vee told us,

"The next place has a beautiful view." They went on foot down to the beach road and started to walk along.

"Here," said Madame Dee, suddenly. It seemed bright and clean but as they entered several girls were already eyeing- up Rob. They looked at the eating area. It was just a back yard adjacent to the bar, which was clearly the main business. All three turned away.

"Sure the sea is beautiful, but this place is just booze and sex – it's the style of trade around here!"

"Ok, one more place," Vee said, remembering her mum said 3. Madame Dee spoke to Vee.

"My mum is sorry, not found yet. We go now on pick-up along the sea front." Then following Madame Dee they walked up the road. They came to a sort of garden with lights. It was on a corner. There were plenty of tables. A few doing business. There was also the interior of the restaurant and an upstairs area- all with air conditioning! The lighting was stylish. The owner came to Madame Dee. He was an elderly Thai man. Vee and Rob liked this restaurant. They could imagine themselves sitting there, eating. Rob picked up a menu and showed it to Vee.

"Just a minute," she said –

"Horng nam yu ti nai?" she asked the elderly Thai man. He replied and she went off. Some minutes later Vee returned.

"I have just been to the Ladies' room. It seems ok. It was reasonably clean and there was toilet paper. There was also a basket and a small wash basin, with mirror and an old piece of soap." Vee looked again at the menu.

"Well what then?" Madame Dee asked with a smile on her face.

"Let's find out how much," Vee replied in Thai. She then repeated it in English.

"Good thinking," Rob said. Madame Dee then chatted with the elderly Thai man

"Don't worry, my mother knows what she is doing,"

Vee assured Rob and spoke again to her mother in Thai. Her mother replied to Vee.

Rob knew from his faith in Vee, that this must be the right decision.

Vee spoke again to Rob.

"My mother asks you to come with her tomorrow to a lawyer, because she wants this restaurant, 47, South Pattaya Road to be in our two names."

"Please tell your mother that I am very grateful to her taking that expense upon herself." he said to Vee.

"Sure, but, right now, I think she wants to go back to the hotel, collect her things and go home," Vee explained.

"Ok, let's all return to our hotel," Rob said to her.

....

They took a taxi and not long after, reached the steps leading up to the revolving door. Madame Dee went straight to her room. Rob and Vee were both rather amazed and glad of a chance to relax in the foyer.

"Our solicitor will tell us when we can move in and take over," Rob said.

CARY SIMMONDS - 1

"By the way," he continued, I have received an email from my brother, Cary. He's a trombonist in GSO (Guildford Symphony Orchestra in England) and apparently they are invited as guest performers at Pattaya Music Festival. They are due here in about two weeks, I think he said."

"Sure, you want to meet him, don't you?"

"Yes, GSO will be playing next Tuesday at the Festival. I checked on-line. So I will go there and find him."

"Why not bring him to meet us?"

"Ok I'll let you know when he will come."

Rob and Vee were in the mood for relaxation after their successful day's work. Remaining at their Hotel they took themselves for a Thai Massage and Steam Sauna. Rob came out first and began his massage. Vee took longer for both. Rob got himself dressed and waited patiently for her. He bought a newspaper and did the Sudoku puzzle. He was just checking the headlines when Vee appeared looking clean and fresh.

"What do you want to do, my love?" Rob asked.

"Up to you," came the automatic reply. Vee didn't dare pressure Rob into a situation with which he wasn't 100% comfortable.

"I think we have earned ourselves an early night,"

"Ok, old man. I don't mind because I old lady!"

They both laughed. They both knew the sleep routine.

Next morning, they went with Madame Dee to her lawyer. The restaurant, ''Rob and Vees'' was put in joint names.

It was a weekend of more swimming. Vee thoroughly enjoyed it. But Rob seemed to feel rather exhausted by it.

ROB AND VEE -2

Vee was very concerned and insisted that he rest. "I can order food and anything you want," she said. But there was a tremor in her voice and tears in her eyes. Rob, she could see, was not well.

"Are you in pain?" she asked.

"Just a little," was his evasive reply. Vee phoned the desk to ask for a doctor. They waited. A doctor came. He examined Rob.

"How old are you Sir?" was his first question.

"59" Rob replied truthfully. The doctor looked at Vee. She glared at him.

"I'll wait in the other room, if you can promise me you'll make him better," she said contemptuously.

"I can't promise that, but I will do my best." Rob was amused to have caused two Thai people to speak English with each other. Vee went into the other suite. As soon as the door shut, her tears flowed – they were tears of fear.

She must not lose Rob.

"He is a father to me and I love him very much,

"Please, Dear God," she prayed, as she had learned from Rob,

"Help dear Rob to regain his strength and vitality. Take this sickness from his body and make him healthy again – please…" she added for good measure. The tears were less now. She wiped her eyes with a towel in the bathroom and looked in the mirror at her puffy face. Suddenly there was a knock on the door.

She opened it and the doctor smiled at her.

"Good news, Just see that he takes this medicine 2 times a day and he should be all right." The doctor handed her a bottle of white stuff. "It's 2 teaspoonfuls 2 times a day."

"Thank you." Rob signed the Doctor's bill. She put the medicine on the dressing table and the doctor went. Rob sat up in bed,

"I feel ok now!" He announced.

"Oh Rob, I was so worried about you," she muttered, snuggling up to him in bed.

"Let's get some food," Rob said, searching about for the room-service menu. Vee handed it to him. She then gave him 2 spoonfuls of medicine. Rob swallowed, then made his choice. Vee glanced at the menu. Rob phoned and ordered for both of them. The food came. It was good and nourishing, just what they both needed. They then got ready to go out.

Rob told Vee he would check his email, for news of his brother. They entered an internet café. Vee asked to check her emails too. Rob was first. Cary would be coming in a few days. He was going to be all the time with the orchestra.

Vee began her email search.

"SooSoo and Jira are getting married," she reported.

"Wow, and I didn't think they were that serious! When is it?"

"Oh, it's tomorrow at Prachin Buri – they cannot have it in Ban Nong Chim because of SooSoo's 'unfavourable reputation' there. Tarrin will go and my mother is expected also.

"I think we should make an effort to see their wedding,"

"Yes, my love, you are right."

. . . .

Vee did not forget Rob's evening medicine. They started the next morning, after breakfast, by limousine for Prachin Buri.

CUTIE'S COOL WEDDING

There was a large crowd and a lot of chatter. Vee's mother arrived. They greeted each other, then a van drew up and some monks got out. They were met by people who took them to a house, that had opened its door to them. Jira looked smart in his formal Thai clothing. Rob shook his hand and wished him good luck and SooSoo wore a blue mudmee saree. Vee, for the first time, spoke to her. SooSoo sounded polite and friendly. It seemed to Vee that Jira had had a sobering effect on her. Prayers were said. Rice was thrown. The happy couple left, in a taxi.

Madame Dee invited Rob and Vee to stay at her place over night. They both accepted graciously. Vee intimated that her mother probably disliked being alone in the house, now that there was a risk of robbery and she had got herself a taste for Bangkok anyway. Some men from the Ban Nong Chim café arrived with a whole assortment of pots and pans. They had been commissioned to bring food for the gathering at the house. Madame Dee dismissed them and brought dishes and cutlery from her kitchen. These were distributed around the table and the dishes placed in the middle. Kao Suay (boiled white rice) came first. Then everybody helped themselves to the other dishes. Madame Dee had evidently set them to task, giving clear orders for what she wanted cooked. The little café had probably earned today more than in the last two weeks. Everyone ate enthusiastically and enjoyed the food. Vee removed something from Rob's dish. "This is too hot for you," she murmured. Rob thanked her. Madame Dee announced, through Vee, that she would be leaving Ban Nong Chim, tomorrow. A lorry would be calling, with men to help lifting and loading. A house in Bang Na was ready and waiting for her to move in.

They passed a pleasant and quiet night at Ban Nong Chim.

"I suppose we'll never see this place again and Tarrin

will be with his mum,"

"That's true - all I know is that you told me to trust your mother's intuition."

"Yes, you are right, my love. But now you have to take your medicine again – I forgot it this morning but once a day is better than not at all." She gave Rob his two spoonfuls, then put it away. Good night."

"Good night my love."

....

The crowing cock announced the new morning in Ban Nong Chim. It was time for Rob and Vee to leave. Vee went to see if her mother was awake. Madame Dee was already up and getting herself ready when Vee reached her.

Vee returned having thanked her and said good-bye.

She gave Rob two spoonfuls of medicine and also informed him that her mother's house would be B106 in Bang Na. (The lawyer had been very helpful to her)

Vee went to get the taxi. It drew up. She and Rob sat in the back. A bag went in the front and the others in the boot.

"Royal Cliff Beach Hotel, Pattaya, please."

"Yes, Sir"

"You ok my love?"

"I'm fine, thank you."

"I must send an email to Cary to see if we can meet, while he's here in Thailand."

"Good idea. I will remind you."

At this time Madame Dee, herself, was in a taxi following a lorry. It was going, all the way, from Ban Ning Chim to Unit B106 in Bang Na Housing Compound. She had dreamed of making this move and now it was a reality. It was a time at which she was both excited and worried.

Rob and Vee, in their taxi, going in the same direction, were getting nearer to Pattaya. As the surroundings became more familiar they both looked forward to the hotel's breakfast buffet. On arrival, they unloaded, paid the taxi and the hotel porters immediately took their baggage.

Only moments later they were both ready for the buffet breakfast. As they were drinking coffees, Rob excused himself to find out where he could check his emails. He was soon sitting, in an alcove, before a screen. Surprise, surprise! He had received another email from Cary. Cary's commitment to GSO will finish 18/07 – 'That's tomorrow!' Rob told himself. Cary went on to say that he was truly amazed by Thailand and as he was finishing with GSO, he was interested in getting a place here in Thailand and asked Rob, *"What do you advise?"*

Rob replied,

"Let's meet, I'm at the Royal Cliff Beach Hotel Pattaya, Suite 42. I'll help you as much as I can. Call the Hotel – they are in the phone book and hope to see you Soon! All the best. Rob"

"Let's stay today, in the hotel," Rob said, when he returned from the Police Station with his newly stamped passport.

"I'll be all right. I just think I should get a bit more rest at the moment."

"No problem, up to you!" They returned to the suite.

CARY SIMMONDS -2

Vee was happy to be exclusively with Rob and able to look after him. She gave him his two spoonfuls of medicine. Vee could see that he was really glad of the rest. It worried her that Rob was getting tired despite taking his medicine. Rob decided to use his time to talk about Cary.

"My younger brother Cary was the brains of the family. When he was 18 he wrote a book, 'How to sight-read music' and got it published. He now gets royalties. He can play the violin and piano, as well as trombone. When he was 21, he joined GSO, which was our local orchestra. I remember hearing them on the radio. He went to practice sessions with groups of friends but his world was quite apart from mine. I was a commuter, taking the train to the City of London every day.

Cary's life was just becoming a routine, when, out of the blue he met Rosita Hirsch. She was, an absolutely charming, German girl - GSO's principal cellist. They fell in love, got married and before we knew it, Rosita was unwell. Doctors attended her at home and said that she was suffering from some sort of virus, but they could not identify it. Poor Cary didn't know whether he was coming or going. GSO put a student trombonist in his place. In just a few weeks, Rosita was no longer of this world. Cary was a changed man."

Rob and Vee realised how lucky they were to be together. They were beginning to get ready to go out, when suddenly the phone rang.

"Hi, is that you Rob?" Vee handed the phone to Rob.

"Hello, this is Rob Simmons, is that Cary?"

"Hello old chap, is it ok if I come at about 3pm this afternoon? I'll wait in the foyer."

"Certainly, Cary, it'll be good to see you. Thanks for calling. Bye!"

"I think we should take him to see 'Rob & Vee's'. We have another meeting next week,"

Later, in the hotel restaurant at lunch –

"I'll have to make a list of the work to be done before we can move in."

"What about paintwork?"

"It depends what we see when we go there, but I am trusting your mother to keep her eye on that kind of thing."

"Yes, my love, you are quite right. She will see that everything is done properly."

At just after 3pm Cary called to say he was in the foyer. They went down. Rob and Cary were about the same height but Cary made Rob look chubby. Cary was not thin, but had no spare flesh on him. He also had dark brown hair. "Well Rob, I can see you haven't been wasting time, May I know who this charming young lady is?" Rob then introduced Vee. Vee smiled.

"Nice to meet you, Cary." Rob then explained the need for their business trip.

"We have another meeting of all partners, next week."

So Rob, Cary and Vee, went to the ground floor.

As they went past their hotel's restaurant, people came and went. It would not close down yet. They sat in the foyer, discussing 'Rob & Vee's'. Rob made his list and Cary suggested some sort of music system – just to help create the right atmosphere.

....

"I am beginning to tire of my routine with GSO. The concerts seem to be usually for the same pieces of music again and again. For some reason, I am no longer surrounded by throngs of friends – at the practices, for example. I continue to play well and with technical correctness, but I no longer have passion. Something in my life is missing. But I must say, my experience of Thailand, has been a tonic to me. This place is fantastic. You were quite right to come here, Rob, you old rogue!"

"I agree with you about Thailand, so you want to get a

place here and – what?"

"Oo, I don't know. May be start a music school?"

"So you'll want to be in Bangkok?"

"Maybe, but first I'll book in here for a while, if you don't mind."

"Be my guest!"

"Oh no, I didn't mean that. It's very kind of you, Rob, but no thank you."

Going to the desk, he said good-bye and Vee found herself giving a dazzling smile, to this honest and kindly man.

Noticing the pool, she was sad that this poor man, Rob, no longer had the energy to go swimming. She was in despair.

"What can I do, Rob, to make you happy? – I'll take off all my clothes and dance, if that's what you want."

"Vee, I know that you would do anything at all for me but what I want, is just to have you here, in this room, with me and feel that you love me as I love you."

"Ok, I will do that, but are you sure that's all?"

"Yes, sure, that's all. And what can *I* do to make *you* happy? Do you want to go to a dancing place or karaoke?"

"No thank you," Vee replied sombrely.

"I just told you. All I want, is to be with you. That's all."

"Ok my love. I understand," he replied, realizing, with sadness, that he was putting pressure on her.

RVC

They returned to their room and Rob rested on the bed. She gave him two spoonfuls of medicine, then sat with him, holding his hand. His face looked relaxed and happy. Vee knew that she would do all in her power to preserve his happiness. She tried to smile but it seemed so difficult. 'Maybe if I don't smile, he will be unhappy,' she thought. She tried really very hard to force herself to smile, but tears came. She blinked and stopped forcing.

"Would you like a tea or coffee?" she managed to say.

"Tea for me, you order what you would like."   She phoned room-service. She put the phone down, then looked at him. He had closed his eyes. 'Always sleeping' she thought. The tea and cappuccino arrived. Vee gave the waiter some money. She noticed that Rob's eyes had just opened.

"Tea's here!" she called. Rob did not move. Vee touched his arm.

"Tea, my love" she repeated. Rob sat up and began to drink.

Vee was worried. 'Would he be able to conduct the meeting in 3 or 4 days' time? More to the point, how long would they have to live like this? Perhaps Rob could take a turn for the better and spring to life again – perhaps not. It occurred to her that she could possibly confide in Cary and pour out her concerns to him. She phoned the front desk, to ask to be put through to him.

"Cary Simmonds – Hello! How can I help you?"

"This is Vee," said the quiet voice on the other end.

"Excuse me? Who's that?"

"I am Vee, who you met yesterday. Your brother, Rob, is sleeping at the moment. I would like to talk to you about him."

"Oh my Goodness – yes, of course – What is your suite number?"

50

"42"

"I'll be over there in just one minute." Hardly had she put the receiver down and tried to compose herself, when there was a knock at the door. She got up and opened it. The man she remembered from yesterday, entered, but as he did so, his eyes followed her.

"I must thank you for doing your best to take care of him."

Cary sat on a chair.

"All Rob does, is lie on the bed and rest. Most of the time, he sleeps. He has no energy to walk anywhere or to go swimming. We just live together in this room."

"I believe he had a heart attack, is that right?"

"Yes, he did, but he recovered."

"That was because you saved his life by calling the hospital immediately – I am very grateful to you for that."

"It was really automatic for me, because I had seen my father die of a heart attack and I knew there was a way to save Rob."

"I cannot thank you enough for saving him."

"What do you think about him now?"

"I'm not sure – you are the one who lives with him.

Perhaps he will thrive on his sedentary lifestyle. May be for years."

"I had to call a doctor yesterday because our trip made him unwell. I have some medicine to give him." Cary looked at her and said,

"You spend all your time with Rob – I think you are in love with him."

"What? He lies in bed and all I do, is sit by him, day after day, and spoon-feed him medicine – you call that love?"

"Yes, certainly, it could be. There are no rules about love. 'It must be like this, this and this' - No, You and Rob, I think I understand." Vee realised that this man was not only good-looking and charming, he was also sensitive.

"Let's go to the restaurant downstairs and have a coffee," Vee recognized the sanity of this voice from the real world.

"Good idea! – one moment."

She spruced herself up as well as possible. Her eyes looked puffy.

"Ok I'm ready!"

They spent a good two hours conversing enthusiastically and promised to meet again.

....

As Vee re-entered the bedroom, something hit her. It was the realization that perhaps she did not love Rob – because Cary – she couldn't get him out of her mind. May be this was Rob's gift to her. Poor Rob. He was always kind. 'Oh I forgot! Rob's medicine' She went to the dressing table, took the spoon and measured it out.

"Come on my dear, It's medicine time!" Rob did his best to rouse himself and was prepared when Vee gave him a spoonful and then another. A mass of conflicting thoughts troubled Vee. She wanted to be faithful to Rob. She had told other boys that she was 'married' to put them off. Here she was, not doing any 'putting off.' Cary could see, quite plainly, her situation. He was waiting for her, somewhere. She could feel it somehow. But what about her faith in Rob?

She dared not tell him her doubts. It was clear to her that Rob was now heavily dependent on her. He couldn't function without her. There was just one more day within these four walls and then it would be, the meeting. 'The best thing for Rob is medicine and rest,' she told herself. Vee knew *she* was getting weaker because of lack of food, but she would be ok until breakfast tomorrow.

Next morning, they were both awake. She phoned for tea and coffee, as before. Vee enjoyed her cappuccino. Rob asked what she ate last night.

"I wasn't very hungry," she lied.

"You should have ordered something." Vee got herself washed and dressed. When she emerged, Rob followed.

They went down for the buffet breakfast. Vee was eager to get something, but she couldn't escape from worry about Rob. Just breakfast, was a precarious event for Rob. Her worries were calmed as Rob took his favourite muesli and other things, then began to talk.

"I've been giving you a hard time recently," Rob began. Vee had nearly finished her rice soup and wanted something more.

"Really?" she said, swooping off to get eggs on toast with tomatoes on toast. "It's really quite an easy job, you know, looking after you. I hope you think I'm doing it properly." She dug in to her breakfast.

"You are doing it perfectly, but I am making too much demand on you."

"Sorry, Rob, I don't agree. It's not your fault when you are unwell and it's my job to see that you are properly looked after."

"But it's unnatural for a girl like you, to be all the time with an invalid old man, like me."

"May be, but I told you, I like the job – it's the best one I have ever had." Breakfasts were coming to an end. They both got up and moved to the lounge.

"By the way, Rob, don't forget to phone everyone about tomorrow. I'll make all the Thai calls for you." She called Lek.

"He will come with Prem and Tan." Next she called her mother. She would come with Tarrin. Jira would make his own way. Thus a useful morning's business was concluded.

"What about Cary?"

"Oh Cary! Yes, good idea. I'm sure he'll find it interesting."

"Well, why not invite him?"

"Ok," Rob called him. He explained to Cary about his business plan and invited him to the meeting.

Cary said he would be busy, so not able to make it, but thanked Rob for thinking of him. Vee was glad that Rob had handled that so smoothly.

Rob and Vee then went to ''Indian by Nature','' for

their own private lunch. Vee was glad that Rob now seemed to have some energy and was up to going places and doing things. 'I am back with my Rob again! The prayers must have worked!' 'Indian by Nature' was the delight they expected it to be. Rob and Vee were both pleased to be back chatting and enjoying food together. They mentioned, that they would be arriving with 8 more people, the next day. It was soon time to go. They returned to the massage and Sauna place. Vee booked a Sauna and massage but Rob, just a massage. Afterwards, Vee's phone rang. It was her mother.

"My mum has seen our new place and it's ready for us now, let's phone everyone and tell them to meet there."

"No, not yet, I'll give them the option of lunch first, if they want it. As soon as we're ready we'll go there. Ok, but, we still have to get the decorators in, to give the place a makeover."

Rob and Vee returned to their hotel. There was in interesting documentary programme about elephants in Thailand, on the TV in the lounge, so they sat and watched. Tiredness gradually overcame them both. They left the documentary programme and returned to their room. They spent a night, both happy to be close to each other.

....

The morning found this well-rested twosome up a little later than was their habit. They both moved faster than usual. It was the day of the big meeting. They both got ready and went together to breakfast. Rob tried rice soup.

"They don't make it hot here."

Vee tried muesli with milk. It was like Rob and Vee in the old days!

It was time to spruce up and check they had everything for the meeting. Rob and Vee had everything ready. She gave him his two spoonfuls of medicine. They sat in their room and relaxed.

"Did you know Tarrin teaches Muay Thai (Thai Boxing?)."

"No, I had no idea!"

"Well, he's doing very well, I have heard."

"Oh, I am very pleased for him, he's a very capable young man."

"Ok it's time!" Vee was pleased to hear Rob as sharp as his old self.

Armed with their briefcases, they took a limousine to 'Indian by Nature'.

BUSINESS MEETING - PREP

Gradually, the expected crowd gathered.

"Well do we all stand here getting ourselves roasted or go inside or go somewhere else – what's it to be?" Hardly had Rob finished speaking, when there was a general surge towards the doors of 'Indian by Nature'. The decision had been made. Uniformed men promptly held the doors open for them and they entered the cool simulated jungle, with quiet sitar and tabla music. Menus were consulted and juices with non-alcoholic sangria were passed around.

It was quite as delightful as expected. There were dishes and bowls with tarka dhal, vegetable jal farazi, rogan josh, aloo saag and brinjal bhajee. There were also, dishes of sambols and various plates with chapattis. Steaming rice arrived. Everyone enjoyed themselves. Rob started to talk about the work he wanted done in the new place.

"Don't worry Mr. Rob, I know how to fix workers and what needs doing" Vee's mother told her in Thai. Rob was intrigued by Vee's translation. As plates were cleared some Indian Sweets arrived – there were ledou, barfi, rasgulla, gajjar ka halwa, gulab jamon and a sprinkling of jalebis. With that, coffees came. It was the perfect ending to a perfect meal.

Rob and Vee with Vee's mother, were the first to leave.

Taking a leisurely pace, they stepped outside and the doorman commandeered them a taxi. Rob gave him some money and he received it politely. Soon they were speeding on their way to South Pattaya Road.

As they pulled up, it was obvious work had already started. There were ladders, buckets and men all over the shop and some outside. There was the sound of a powerful drill at work somewhere within the building. Men called out to each other. Madame Dee said something to Vee.

"They all know what needs to be done. They are

working for my mother. She hired them."

"Something else I have to thank you for. It would have taken weeks for me to find guys to work like this." Vee translated. Her mother replied to her. She said,

"I want to help this business to get started. It will be ready by the weekend."

"Ok we've all seen what is going on here and we have Madame Dee to thank for that."

Next Monday – early that's 9 am I want you all here to start work. – You will find out on Monday exactly what that means in your case. So thanks for coming and goodbye for now."

This was the signal for everyone to make their own way home. Rob hailed a taxi and told the driver "Bang Na." He beckoned to Madame Dee. She thanked him and got in. The taxi sped off. Lek and the lads went off together. Rob and Vee said their good-byes and took a taxi to the Royal Cliff Beach Hotel.

TARRIN AND ORN - 1

Also, at about this time, Tarrin's day off from work came round again. He always looked forward to the Thai Boxing School. He had some good, enthusiastic, lads who had fights together regularly. Naturally, he was always keen to welcome prospective new boxers. One morning he had quite a surprise as a couple of girls turned up. They made it quite clear that they were there to improve their boxing skill. Tarrin had always considered himself broad-minded, but somehow the idea of 2 girls bashing and kicking hell out of each other, jarred against all the assumptions he had ever made about females. He had to admit they were good fighters and he was glad to have them in his school. One, in particular, attracted his interest. When they had finished their session and taken a shower, he spent time talking with the attractive one. The other one said, 'Good-bye.'

Tarrin found himself with someone who apparently had time and interest in talking to him. They exchanged names. She was 'Orn.' She had grown up since the age of about 5 without a mother or father and she knew that to survive in this world, she had to be hard and tough, so she needed Muay Thai, to help her adapt. Tarrin listened to her and said,

"What if you had someone who wanted to love you and take care of you?"

She laughed,

"I think you have been watching too many movies."

"No, actually, I never watch movies, but I know I would like to take care of you." "Get away from me, you talking like that – just for stupid girls!" she said angrily.

"No, I don't want a stupid girl, I want a strong one like you, who needs someone to take care of her."

"You don't know me. Why you think I want you?"

"You are a very good fighter but when you come out of the ring you can stop fighting. Not all life is a fight."

"You say that because you had easy life, with mama

and papa to do everything for you. Well – I had no mama and no papa!" she added as tears appeared in her eyes. Tarrin went towards her, intending to hold her.

"Keep off from me and remember, I am a Muay Thai fighter."

"Me too. But that doesn't mean, you and me have to fight."

"What's the matter with you – you don't know me, so what you want from me?"

"I don't know much about you, but what I know, I think I understand – and I find you very attractive."

"You have bad eyes. I'm not attractive – I am just plain Orn – that's me."

"No, my eyes are A1 and I don't agree with you. 'Plain' is not a word to describe you."

"You want me here all night talking to you like this?"

"If you can stay, yes. I want you to be with me."

"How do you know I will not fight you?"

"I just take that risk. I don't intend to give you any reason for fighting me."

"Or, real fancy talker you are. But crazy."

"You will stay with me then?"

"What mobile you?" They exchanged mobile numbers and she left.

On his next day off, Tarrin called Orn.   This is the translation –

"Hello, is that Orn?"

"Well, who do you think it is?"

"I am so pleased it's you. I want to invite you to lunch today."

"You what? You are mad."

"I'll take you to the place where I work."

"What? You work in a restaurant?"

"That's right. Will you come?"

"Why you want me to come?"

"Because I love you."

"Because what?"

"Because I love you."

"Yes."

"Yes – what?"

"Yes, I'll come - where is the restaurant?" Tarrin told her and they actually agreed, it would be 1 o'clock. Tarrin arrived at 12.45. Everyone was surprised to see him on his day off. He just said he would be, "having lunch with a friend." He spent a moment chatting with Jira and SooSoo. Suddenly the door opened. It was Orn. She managed a smile. Tarrin escorted her to a table and handed her a menu. They both made a selection and ordered. Talk was about food and cooking. Orn was surprised that Tarrin knew so much about it. He dismissed it as 'his job.' They then had a dessert followed by a coffee. Tarrin explained that this place was his livelihood when not at the gym. Orn asked where he lived and he found some embarrassment in saying that he lived with his mother.

"You must come and meet her," seemed to Tarrin, to be the only thing he could say. On this occasion, Orn did not seem to be in fighting mode, so they made a date. Tarrin called his mother and said he would come with a friend,

"Yes, bring her along, you'll both be very welcome." That same evening Tarrin arrived at his mother's Bang Na house with Orn. Tarrin explained to Orn that his mother was a clairvoyant and healer.

"Well, my dear," she began to Orn, "I can see that your life has been full of pain – I don't know how you have managed to live with it, but obviously you are extremely brave, to be able to come here now.   Now, you, my lad want love, from her. The only way, is to give her all the love you can – Just give love – give love and give love – then, she will love you. But remember, she cannot love you immediately, because of her pain."

"Thank you mother, I am very grateful to you."

"Thank you Mam, you are very kind. May be one day, your words true!"

It was the best day off, Tarrin had ever had.

But, yet another day off, was devoted to Orn. She said

she worked in a souvenir shop, but it didn't make much money. He took Orn to a Thai Restaurant that his mother told him about.

"Why don't you change your job? You could soon learn the job where I work and everyone would be glad to have you on the staff."

"You're giving me a bit of strong talk, I would say."

"I am telling you the absolute truth. I would never tell you a lie."

"Ok, now *I* will tell *you* the absolute truth. I learned, at a very early age, not to believe anything, from a man like you."

"But I am not one of those men."

"Oh yeah? Just who do you think you are – Mr Fancy talker?"

"I am a man who loves you."

"You can't be. I am a fighter."

"I am in love with you and remember – my mother said you are in pain – that means emotional pain."

"Well, what are you gonna do about it?" Tarrin stood up. He opened his arms. "Come here," he said.

"What? You want to fight?"

"No, just trust me, for God's sake." She stepped towards him and he hugged her. She then used her arms to encircle him. Their eyes were closed. As they parted, Tarrin said, "I love you." Orn sat down and gazed up into his eyes.

"You LOVE me? You really do love me?"

"YES!" Tarrin replied in quite a loud voice. Orn buried her face in her hands and burst in to tears.

"Do you promise you will never stop loving me, please?" Tarrin was embarrassed to notice that Orn was wetting herself.

"Yes, I promise. I promise I will NEVER stop loving you."

"Oh God – What have I done?" Tarrin asked for the Bill.

"Sorry we have to go, I forgot to turn the oven off." He

gave the waiter money saying,

"Keep the change," and rushed off with Orn.

"It's ok. I'll be alright," Orn said, even though her jeans showed a large wet patch. Luckily, the light was fading. Tarrin could do no more than get a taxi and take her home to mother, so he asked for Bang Na. Finding the house in darkness, "My mum's out," he announced. As he inserted the key, he turned to Orn, Go in and go straight on. My room is at the end," he said, switching on the lights. "That's my room in there and that's the bathroom. Orn was able to strip off and have a shower.

The best Tarrin could do, was offer her the loan of pair of his under-pants and jeans. Not the latest fashion for a lady, but much better than what she had. Tarrin sat on the bed and waited patiently. He gazed at a photo of Bangkok on the wall. When comfortably dressed, Orn kissed him. He put the clothing items, she had discarded, in a plastic bag. Orn said she lived at Lat Phrao. They went outside. He got her a taxi and agreed the fare.

"See you tomorrow at work?"

"Ok," she said, as the taxi sped off.

Next day, Orn gave him a bag with some of his own clothes, and their eyes met. Soon Orn became accepted as a useful member of staff and she began to feel more comfortable with Tarrin. He was always easy with her and gentle. She began to open her heart to him. They arranged to get a place so that they could live together. Tarrin found an apartment they could easily afford to rent, for a while. They bought their own towels, bedsheets and pillowcases. Some items for the kitchen were also needed.

On his next day off Tarrin took Orn to the Thai restaurant at the Landmark Hotel. She was very impressed, to be in such a grand establishment. They looked forward to lying in bed together for a kiss and cuddle. Only one snag, it was the kind of air-conditioner whose noise you just had to get used to.

"Don't worry, in a few months I'll buy a condo for us." Tarrin assured her.

They decided on breakfast in a street restaurant. Orn asked him how much he was paid. She was keen to start work with him to try to improve her financial situation. She felt she could make a success of it, so long as Tarrin was there.

When Tarrin's next day off came the only girl to come to the gym was Orn. She was not there for Muay Thai. Tarrin put his lads through their fights. As soon as they had finished he turned to Orn and made a lunch date with her.

His mother had invited them both to The Landmark. They went to the Thai restaurant there. It was a moment of luxury for Tarrin and Orn

Tarrin bought a Condo and invited Orn to move in with him as soon as her last rent was paid. Orn began to feel more comfortable with Tarrin.

NOON and LEK

Noon didn't feel confident enough to become a regular, with a gang of young people, working in a restaurant. Lek was very easy-going and accepted how she felt about it. He was aware that Noon's sense of self-esteem, needed some repair work, and he was sure Noon was capable of far more than she realized. He knew she enjoyed the food at 'Rob & Vee's.' Noon had spent many years of her life as a nurse in a Bangkok Hospital, so was not averse to hard work.

But it seemed to her, as she told Lek, that she had less energy, nowadays. Lek recommended a herbal remedy to her and Noon was very grateful. He was invited to share Noon's apartment. He agreed to visit her on a trial basis. She had a way of letting him know that she couldn't oblige him at the moment owing to it being the time of her – 'you know, like all women every month.'

Lek replied.

"Yes, sure, ok. No problem. It just means you are fitter and healthier than you thought you were."

"Does it? I don't know what I thought." Lek laughed.

"Don't worry, if you should forget, I can put ideas into your head."

"Or, you bad man!"

"No – good ideas – good man!" They went to a Thai Restaurant. "This Patakhan Thai!" (haute couture Thai cuisine) Noon was suitably impressed. It was the first time she had entered such an establishment. The food delighted both of them. They drank coconut juice. The rice was of two colours. The bowls of various concoctions were delightful.

"Se Beau?" Lek asked,

"Seb Yu" replied Noon. "How did you know I am from Isan?"

"I just guessed. You have an Isan smile," he added.

"Or, really?" Lek found Noon very relaxing to be with.

She, no doubt, thought the same about him. Noon said she wanted Lek to visit her family in her village. She told him the name of the village.

"I don't think it's on any map," she explained. "Many Thai villages are known, only to people who live in, or come from them. Villagers are regarded as the poor underclass of Thai people. They do not get the full benefit of municipal services in villages. Each village has a 'Poo Yai Ban' a sort of Local Chief, who maintains the status quo."

Lek, who came originally from the Bangkok area, was intrigued, to learn how different, life in Thai villages was. The nearest town was Buriram – a well-known town in Isan. You then take the Surin Road to Kilo 9 and turn off right. I will show you."

Lek took time off from 'Rob & Vee's', as did Noon. They went together up-country. A train from Bangkok's Hualumphong Station took them to Buriram. They arrived the next day. It was just a lot of sitting on plain wooden seats and waiting. They called into a place in Buriram to get some food, then bought some items to carry home. Lek followed Noon's suggestions. They got a Tuk-Tuk and Noon negotiated the price. They shot off up the road towards Surin. Suddenly the little truck turned right, on to a footpath, through the jungle. It didn't seem to slow down at all. It went on and on until it came to a clearing and some houses. "Welcome to my village," Noon said. She told the driver where to stop. They got out and Lek followed Noon into a house. It was hot and there was quite a bit of litter about. In the house it was much more comfortable. They sat on the floor and it was cooler. Lek was presented to Noon's Mother, then Noon's sister. They all drank tea together and Noon opened a packet of nuts and candy, she had bought in Buriram, to pass round to everyone. Noon told her mother that they now worked in a restaurant in Pattaya and many farangs went to it. Maybe you can find a husband for Pla? (Noon's sister)

"I don't know about a husband, but I can get her a job,"

Lek responded. Pla seemed to be a teenager, eager to escape the tedium of her home environment, like teenagers everywhere.

"She'll have to learn English, of course."

"I can speak English," Pla said, in English.

"That's good! How old are you?"

"Seventeen, eighteen next week"

"Come back with us, then?" they continued, in Thai. They were then shown their way about the house – where they could wash and where they could sleep. Everyone dispersed – some to other houses, some to the back of this house, one went to his motorbike and drove off. Soon there was quiet, apart from the incessant sound of insects, the occasional squawk, or distant whistle, of a tropical bird. These were the sounds familiar to the Isan night.

They left Isan the next morning. Noon gave her mother some money. A taxi appeared and drove them to Buriram. They were just in time for the train to Bangkok. They arrived at Hualumphong, tired and very hungry, they took a taxi and told the driver they were hungry so,

"Please stop where there is a restaurant in business, but our aim is to get to Pattaya." Noon gave him the address. Soon they were sitting in a busy café – restaurant, on the road to Pattaya. They were able to serve themselves and took ample portions of vegetarian food. They ate hungrily, enjoying it, and gaining strength as they proceeded. They returned to the taxi, feeling much better. In less time than expected, they were 'home' – at Noon's apartment.

"Well, as you are here, why don't you come in?"

"Thank you for inviting me." Lek followed her in. They all had luggage. "Come in here." Lek entered as he was bidden. Noon showed him where to dump his luggage and offered him a comfortable seat. Pla also found a seat.

"Tea, coffee, juice?" There was a small table. Lek asked for 'Nam Som' (orange juice). Noon took an iced coffee, as did Pla.

"You could stay here, if you want to."

"Want to what? – You mean that you could satisfy

66

ANYTHING I might want, if I stayed here."

"That wasn't quite what I meant – I would like to stay here – but perhaps another time?"

"That door there is my bathroom and toilet. There's where I sleep, but I like a firm mattress."

"Me too."

"You'll have to come and give me your opinion on *my* place."

"Ok." Lek excused himself, picked up his luggage and said ,

"Good-bye, just for now - if you give me your number, I'll call you."

Lek was ready with pen and notebook. She announced it to him.

"Ok, thanks for the orange juice."

"You're welcome." Next day, Lek called.

"Hello is that Noon?"

"Hello Lek, how are you?"

"Ok thanks – Do you have my number now?"

"Yes, of course."

"Well, get a taxi, phone me again and give him your phone. I will give him directions to my place."

"Ok." Lek called 'Rob & Vee's' to say that he and Noon could not be in to work tomorrow. His phone rang as soon as he had finished. It was the taxi driver. Lek gave him directions, then waited. The doorbell rang. He went out to the taxi and paid the driver. Noon smiled at him and thanked him. She and Pla entered, each holding a small bag. Noon wore jeans and a blouse. Pla's neat mop of blonde hair bounced as she mounted the stairs. She wore shorts and a tee shirt. Lek could see that Noon was quite agile for her age. Entering his room was quite a shock for Noon. There was a desk, a bed and a table. The table and desk were covered in papers, envelopes, CD's. a beaker of pens and various books. Some clothes were hanged on hangers on the doors of the wardrobe. There was a modest-sized TV and a DVD player. When she had taken in all the clutter, she asked to use the toilet. Lek immediately directed her. When she re-appeared, he said,

"Aren't you tired, after that journey?"

"Yes, very tired."

"No problem, sleep here then. Pla can sleep in the spare room. I'll make it ready for her." Lek checked the bed and switched on the air conditioning. It seemed to be ok. He told Pla and she was glad to get herself installed.

"Sure you don't mind?" Noon asked.

"I would be honoured if you would stay here tonight."

"Wow, well, if you put it like that," she said, leaping on to the bed. Shoes and other clothes soon came off. Lek disrobed similarly. They were both in underclothes as Lek joined her in bed. He sensed that it was still her period. He touched her and her hands felt him. They had a brief peck of a kiss and then said,

"Good Night!"

Tan arrived at work, on time. The door was open and he joined those filing in. Then he noticed a girl running. It was Pla. He greeted her and said,

"Good Morning" They all entered and the new girl, Pla, was introduced to everyone. She was told to spend the day working with Orn. But she seemed to disappear. Orn reported that she couldn't find Pla anywhere. Tan knew exactly where to start *his* job.

SooSoo and Jira were in charge of the daily routines of everyone. The working day began and the first few customers arrived. In about 3 days, another new employee would arrive. Far was looking forward to her new job and being in the same building as Tan all day long. Noon had started to come regularly now and was doing well, learning the job. She also said that she had heard from Pla that she didn't like Bangkok and was going back to her village. Pla told her where she was staying and said she would go in 2 days. Noon took time off, to go and see her. Lek continued to do a good job helping her, as much as he could, with all she needed. She already felt accepted into the 'Rob & Vee's' family of employees and knew that the

Boss was a Farang named 'Mr. Rob'. He was responsible for starting this restaurant that now employed so many people.

Noon found Pla in a bar with some farangs. When she saw her older sister, she acted sick and made an excuse to leave. They went to Pla's room. Noon gave her some money and asked if she was hungry. They went together to a restaurant and Pla ate everything in front of her. Noon then accompanied her back to her room to get her personal luggage and they took a taxi to Hualumpong – Bangkok's Main Railway Station. Noon bought her a ticket for Buriram and the two of them hugged tearfully as she boarded the train. Doors slid closed and it started to move, gradually sliding out of the station, to rattle and shudder over the points and then gather speed. Pla had gone out of Noon's life, but she would be safe now! She went back to tell Lek.

KRABI

"How would you like to spend a week, Rob?" Vee asked.

"Well, I don't know what you mean. It's got to be with you, of course."

"Yes, but we have a week in which to do anything we like. For example, we don't have to stay in Pattaya."

"Where then?"

"Koh Samet or Koh Phi Phi"

"I'd like to stay in that place on the poster you showed me in the Travel Agent shop downtown."

"Oh I think you mean Krabi. Wait I'll show you."

Vee delved into her bag and pulled out a small notebook – her diary. She opened it at the first page and said,

"You mean here?"

"Yes that's it!" "Ok let's checkout. Take all our things and go to Krabi."

"Yes, tomorrow morning, ok?"

"Give me five!"

"What? – Oh, ok!"

They enjoyed their last sleep at the Royal Cliff Beach Hotel.

In the morning, Vee checked her mobile.

"Ok I'll book us Railay Beach Hotel, All right"

"I don't know."

"Look here!" She showed him the pictures of the hotel and surroundings on her mobile.

"Looks nice, you have already booked it?"

"Well I made a reservation but I didn't pay, of course."

"Ok, good, we'll go there. I am sure it will be very nice."

"Quick, we don't want to miss breakfast, before we go."

"We'll be lucky to find a hotel as nice as this one."

"Actually, in Thailand there are an enormous number of amazingly good hotels, so it's quite possible we find one as good as this hotel."

They talked while managing to serve themselves and load their plates with food. Finally, the coffee came. They took it to sit in the lounge.

"Are you quite sure you have packed everything?"

"I think so. What about you, Rob?"   There was a final return to room. Then it was time to check out. Rob paid the Hotel and gave the porters tips.

"Can you go by taxi to Krabi?"

"I think so."   The taxi came and they both sat in the back.

"Krabi please. Railay Beach, ok?"

"Yes Sir! Ok Sir, Krabi!" They held hands.

"We go to Bangkok first, maybe we can stop a while there?"

"Yes, good idea, we better tell the driver."

"Ok we stop in Bangkok for may be one day and continue next day to Krabi, ok?"

"Yes Boss, No problem."

It was evening as they drew into downtown Bangkok. Rob asked for Sukhumvit and soon after, they were there, following the skytrain.

"We would like to go to the Landmark Hotel," he told the driver.

When they arrived, it was Monday evening. Vee spoke to the driver in Thai.

"I told him we would probably be ready for him again on Wednesday morning but please check with me tomorrow – I gave him my number."

"Thank you." Rob went with Vee to check in. Their luggage was waiting for them on a trolley. They were escorted to their room and then the luggage arrived. Rob tipped the two porters and closed the door.

"Well, at least it's different Rob!"

"Yes I think you were right. We needed a change."

They began unpacking.

"Don't unpack much because we're going on from here."

In their Landmark Hotel room, Rob and Vee both

managed a shower and change of clothes. Downstairs in the Coffee Shop, nothing had changed. Rob invited Vee to the Thai restaurant, adjacent to the coffee shop. She, refused.

"I want you to have the kind of food you enjoy." So they diverted to the Coffee Shop.

"Mushroom quiche, for you Rob?"

"Oh, you can say it properly now!" The waiter came, Rob ordered,

"Two mushroom quiches, please"

"With side-salads sir?"

"Yes, please." Vee copied Rob and put mustard and ketchup on her quiche. When she tasted them her face screwed up.

"Never mind if you don't like them."

The next experiment was mayonnaise on the salad. Vee put just a very small blob. She tried it with a piece of tomato. Her decision was 'better without it,' and she just left it on her plate. Rob watched all the time, thinking, 'I suppose English junk food won't get very far in Thailand.'

"Did you like the quiche?"

"Yes - aroy maak, ka"

"What's that mean?"

"Delicious."

"That's good. What about a cake with your coffee?"

"Ok, I get you mille feuille, it's French it means something like a thousand sheets, there is cream between them."

"What about you, Rob?"

"I will have chocolate éclair it's a kind of long bun with chocolate on top and cream in the middle" Rob took them to the table. They started with great enthusiasm and the coffees arrived. Rob had a café au lait and Vee had her usual cappuccino.

"Oh dear! I have forgotten your medicine, Rob. We must do it as soon as we go back upstairs." They continued in their little heaven while it was still there on the plate.

Back in the room Vee realised that Rob's medicine had almost run out. But she also noticed that he seemed to be ok. Vee's phone rang. It was the taxi driver checking with them.

"I think we go tomorrow morning about 9.30, is that ok with you, Rob?"

"10 o'clock will be better." Vee told the taxi driver and it was settled.

"Well I think that so far our little trip has been a great benefit to us both."

"You are quite right, my love, let's hope we enjoy Krabi too." They spent a comfortable night.

In the morning sun poured in through the curtains. Rob had the last of his medicine. They got packed then went down to the breakfast buffet. They had quiche with spinach and tomato. There was marmalade or honey for the toast. Vee tried honey. Rob's preference was the good quality marmalade provided by the Landmark. They finished with coffees.

"Excuse me sir, your taxi is here," a uniformed bellboy told them. They wandered down to reception. Their bags were waiting for them. Rob checked out and they went to the taxi. Rob tipped the lads with their bags.

"Good morning Sir. Good morning Miss," the taxi driver said to them,

"We go now to Krabi, ok na?"

"Yes please." He started the cab and they joined the stream of traffic. Rob began to doze and leaned on Vee's shoulder. Vee watched the route. She had not been before to Hua Hin or Cha Am. When eventually these places were reached the taxi sped straight through.

"I think you stop at Prachuap Khiri Khan, there is a big café there where you can relax, watch TV, eat lunch," the driver informed them.

"Ok, good idea."

Rob started to fall off Vee's shoulder and woke up.

"Oh, I'm sorry," he said, realizing what he had done.

"It's all right. I don't mind. You can lie across my lap if

you are tired," Rob then lay down again. The taxi arrived in Prachuap Khiri Khan. The driver parked outside the café with a bus and some cars.

"Rob, my love, we are at a stopping place. We can get food here and there are toilets," she added considering her own feelings. Rob roused himself and slowly opened his eyes.

"Ok, let's go then." The driver watched them leave the taxi and locked up. Vee and Rob entered. It was quite crowded, but there were places and food was being served. It was not particularly cool and there were huge ceiling fans in operation.

"Excuse me, I'm going to the toilet."

"Oh yes, ok, me too." It was not as clean as they had been accustomed to in the hotel.

When they both re-appeared, next on the agenda was food. It was all Thai. Vee spoke to them. She got food for herself and for Rob. They went to sit.

"This is real Thai food, this is how people in my country live." Rob looked at her.

"It's your culture."

"Yes but they are all desperately poor. This is a big day out for most of them here." Rob enjoyed his food and so did Vee. The noise of Thai chatter continued all around them. They finished with 'lot tong' and coffees, which came together. The driver was waiting for them so they left the hubbub of the café and ventured out into the hot air. Their taxi was soon ready to zoom off. They followed the coast road. At Surat Thani they left the coast road. They were in the middle of a bustling town. The driver asked a few people for the road to Krabi and they were Soon on the way again.. Rob and Vee were both attentive to everything around them. It was a mountainous road and it seemed to be in a park. They eventually descended and reached the Krabi road, turning right.

"Nearly there," the driver said. He took them to Railay Beach.

"What Hotel do you want?"

"Railay Beach Hotel,"

"Oh, that's just here!" Rob paid the taxi driver and gave him a tip for good service. Uniformed staff came from the hotel and took the luggage. Rob and Vee walked in, as if they were local governors. They checked in and booked a room on the ground floor with a sea view. Rob and Vee were in Paradise. They could sit on the beach with a coconut, or paddle in the warm turquoise sea. It was all super-clean and the air was fresh.

"Well, we just have a few days here, Rob, because of our job."

"I know, my love, don't worry, I won't forget.

Having changed for the beach, they both went out in to the tropical heat again. They had a frolic and splash in the warm sea. Rob started wading out as it was so shallow. Vee followed. Gradually the depth increased.

"Well, are you going to swim then?"

"Oh all right. I'll try." Vee began her usual thrashing routine and then began to swim more calmly.

"It's easier in the sea!"

"Yes, I know. That's why I asked you to do it. Try swimming on your back." Vee tried. She was surprised that she floated so easily, but moved very slowly. They splashed each other and then began to wade back. They entered the cool hotel draped in towels and soon picked up their keys. In the room they both showered and dressed for lunch.

Surprisingly, it was another buffet, but quite interesting, nevertheless.

"I'm so glad we came here,"

"Me too, It was a stroke of genius, Rob, for which you must take credit."

"Credit taken, thank you, I shudder to think what might have become of us had we not done this."

"Let's not think about that – how's your food?"

"It's a funny mixture of Thai and western."

"Yes, that's what I thought, still it will keep us alive."

"Actually I think I preferred the lunch at Prachuap Kiri Khan," Vee admitted.

"What's the yellow stuff with the fruit?"

"That's custard, it's a sort of mixture of yellow-coloured cornflour, with sugar, milk and vanilla." Vee tried it but was not enthusiastic.

"As we are here for another 24 hours we had better go out and look around the town, there might be a local place where we can eat. We have to book a taxi anyway." So after lunch the two intrepid holidaymakers, made their tentative way towards downtown Krabi. The first place they located was the taxi office. Here Vee asked about a restaurant. Rob booked the taxi back to Bangkok and Pattaya.

"The best restaurant in Krabi is just down here on the left," Vee announced. They called in. Vee had Som-tam and Rob had Rice Soup. Vee asked them to leave out the chilli. It was fairly busy with local people.

"We come here for all our meals. That hotel is no good for food – ok?"

"Yes, good idea, but more expensive for you, Rob."

"Don't worry about that. I just want to be sure we both get proper food, that's all."

"Isn't it funny, most of these people here probably envy us staying at that luxury hotel. They probably think we're stark raving mad coming here to eat!"

"Yes, very funny, ha ha!"

"I mean, funny peculiar – odd, strange, weird."

"I was just joking!"

"Oh sorry, ha ha!" They finished their food and got coffees in paper cups.

"Well that was a productive afternoon's work," Rob said, as they made their way back to the hotel.

"Ah, so nice to be cool again!" – That was what they were missing – The air conditioning!

In rooms it was time to rest and may be watch TV. Rob

put on BBC. Vee took a rest. When Vee got herself up again, Rob was dozing, so she switched off the repetitive jingle from the TV. When she had emerged from the bathroom, Rob was still dozing. She gave him a little shake.

"Are you all right my love?"

"Yes, of course I am!" he said, suddenly springing to life. Vee was glad, but taken by surprise.

"I think you are doing too much."

"Don't worry your little head about me, I'm fine!" The hotel was better than they expected in the evening. They had some fruit, papaya - and strawberries from Chiang Mai. After this little indulgence, they were both ready for bed.

Next morning, the two were up early. The sun rising on the sea was beautiful. Rob and Vee made their way downtown and called in to their eating place. There were only a few people having breakfast at this hour. Rob and Vee found a table with a view of the sea. Rob took up a breakfast menu.

"Rice soup for me and som-tam for you, right?"

"I think I'll have rice soup today." Vee went to get them. Hers was hot and Rob's soup was not hot. They began to put their spoons to use.

"Hey this is a bit hot – you try it!" Vee tried it. Vee's bland-tasting soup was actually meant for Rob, she realised. Then she swapped them round.

"Sorry I got them mixed up." But she knew that it was the cook serving who got them mixed up, not her. Vee would never get something for Rob mixed up. They proceeded to enjoy their breakfasts. Coffee was next. Rob got two paper cups full of steaming coffee. There was milk and sugar on the table.

"Today – I mean, this morning – we say good-bye to Krabi. It has been just what we needed, coming here."

"I am so happy you brought me here, Rob" They left their gradually warming café and walked back to their hotel. It was hot and the morning had come to life. They got themselves ready and packed, then went to the foyer. The taxi was due in 20 minutes

"Good-bye beautiful beach,"

"Well, Pattaya has a beach too."

"But not like Krabi."

"You should go to Koh Larn."

"Mr. Simmonds, Sir – Taxi, Sir" They immediately took their small bags and their luggage followed them out to the taxi. Rob tipped the porters. They had a different driver now. He was a younger man who smiled a lot. He put their luggage in the boot.

"We might stop in Bangkok, but we go to Pattaya" Vee translated.

"Ok, Sir, Stop Bangkok, maybe – understand." Rob smiled at his attempted English. He started up. The taxi seemed to be quite new. The engine wasn't noisy and it had good air conditioning. They were Soon in Surat Thani and began following the coast road.

It was mid-afternoon when they found themselves in the Bangkok part of Sukhumvit.

"Landmark Hotel, please."

"Ok, Sir."

"We have 2 or 3 hours here. Can you wait for us?"

"No problem. I go to Landmark car park."

Rob and Vee, took themselves up the steps like arriving royalty. It was their very own, much-loved, Landmark Coffee Shop. They selected a table and watched the life around them. From his seat Rob could see the Book Shop (Asia Books), the door to the outside tables and street.

The waitress came.

"Well, I would like mushroom quiche,"

"With side salad?"

"Yes, please."

"Same for me, please."

"Thank you Sir, thank you Mam." With their coffees, Rob had a Danish pastry and Vee chose a cake called 'opera.'

Following this pleasant break, there was just time for a

look around the bookshop. Rob bought a copy the Financial Times, feeling it had news with which he should catch up. Vee bought a cartoon paper in Thai.

"Or! - Hallo Sir! Hallo Mam! I wait for you now, ok, na?" The taxi driver looked as though he had been sleeping, but he was not late. They went to the car park and down to the basement. The driver opened the taxi for them and so began their stage 2 journey. He was soon out of the depths of the car-park and on to Sukhumvit Highway coming up to the U-turn filter. It would be only an hour or so to Pattaya now.

"Where you stay in Pattaya, Sir?"

"Royal Cliff Beach Hotel."

"Oh very nice Sir. I take you there."

Sure enough, they reached the Hotel. Rob paid the driver and gave him a tip. The porters came to take their luggage. It was evening. They checked in and were offered the same suite.

"Oh. Here we are again, but tomorrow we start work – 9 o'clock!" They were soon unpacked and ready for bed.

BUSINESS IN-SITU -1

Next morning they were both up early. Vee put on a magenta sari and wore the brooch Rob had given her. Rob wore his dark grey suit and old-school tie. They were soon over breakfast and the limousine swooped off with them down to South Pattaya Road. As they arrived, another taxi drew up. It was Madame Dee in a stunning viridian sari. Madame Dee opened the restaurant then gave the key to her daughter, before leaving. They entered. Two more taxis drew up. It was Lek with Tan and Prem. The other taxi was with Vee's 2 brothers, plus Orn, Tarrin and Jira. A third figure in a turquoise sari, emerged from the taxi, as Tarrin was paying the driver. It was SooSoo, Jira's wife.

"She was interested to come."

"She's welcome to join us." SooSoo and Vee started chatting in Thai.. Tarrin presented Orn and introduced her to everyone. Orn's sari was pale yellow. She had borrowed it.

"Right, Prem I want you in the kitchen. You haven't seen it before. Familiarise yourself with it."

Vee translated. Prem went.

Lek, this is the dining room – where you see all these chairs and tables. You move between here and the kitchen, where Prem went.

"Find the crockery and cutlery." Vee translated again.

"Tan and Jira, you go into the kitchen with Prem and learn the job from him. Your boss is Prem, ok?"

"Yes, ok, thank you Sir."

"Ok Sir."

"SooSoo, I want you, Tarrin and Orn, to help Lek taking orders, between dining rooms and kitchen."

....

"So, Tan and Jira in the kitchen. Tarrin and SooSoo in the dining area as waiters. But only one learner at a time. So – :

Today is day 1

Day 1 Jira with Prem and Orn with Lek. SooSoo and Jira –off! Tarrin Cash-Till

Tomorrow

Day 2 Tan with Prem and SooSoo with Lek - Orn and Tarrin –off! Jira Cash-Till

Day 3 Jira with Prem - SooSoo with Tarrin, Tan and Lek –off! Orn Cash-Till

And so on. Got it?" – Is everybody ready?" Swaps are ok if done in advance.

"Vee, my love, will you be on the cash till, please, with Tarrin?" Rob noticed that Prem already had several things cooking.

"Prem I want you to write some rough notes of menus - let me know what you can offer."

"Ok – Hey this fridge is well stocked!" Tan and Tarrin said good-bye to everyone and left.

"Nine o'clock!" Rob called to them.

"Ok have a look and do some menus." Eventually Prem got 6 or 7 menus done. Rob went down each list writing in prices.

"Is there a float in the till?" Rob asked, expecting Vee to tell him.

"The till is empty."

"Ok we are not open yet. We go to the bank for a float."

"Can you get it?" He asked Vee.

"What's a float?"

"Sorry, money for change. Take 10,000, here you are and bring back some notes and bags."

"Yes, I understand now."

"When Vee comes back, we will open. All food will be at half the price shown on the menus, because this is our first day. Tomorrow, we will have printed menus and no half prices." Everybody absorbed these words as they continued working. Vee arrived back and the till was stocked. Rob put the notice on the door to 'Open.'

"By the way, all tips to be put in the tips jar in the kitchen. Tips are for all of us to share, ok?"

"Well, why don't some of us sit down and start eating? Everyone will think we are customers," SooSoo suggested.

"Brilliant, what do we have, Prem?"

"Soup first, then Brown rice and side salad. There are kebabs for the non-vegetarians."

They sat at various tables as if they didn't all know each other and began to eat. Rob switched on a radio and they got some music. Vee opened the door. As she did so, 3 people entered. They found a free table and their order was taken by Lek. SooSoo watched carefully. Prem was very busy in his kitchen and Jira wondered what he could do to help. There were 3 orders for soup and 4 for kebabs with side salad. Prem got Jira cutting tomatoes, washing lettuce and slicing courgettes. The rice was drained and Prem began to share it out. Eventually orders were filled. SooSoo and Lek were able to pick them up. More customers arrived. Lek took their orders of food to the kitchen.

"There are more seats upstairs, sir!" Vee told them, as she followed with cutlery, serviettes and menus. She noticed it had a loudspeaker with the same music as downstairs, to add to the atmosphere. She took their orders with her, down to the kitchen, marked "U" for 'upstairs.'

Vee told SooSoo that,

"These orders are for people sitting upstairs."

"Thank you – by the way, I love your brooch!" she called at Vee, who then flashed her a smile, then returned to her post at the till. Two people were waiting. They both put some coins in the tips jar. There was a pleasant exchange with Vee in Thai, as it was a bargain price. Rob kept a weather-eye on all proceedings. It seemed to him to be working well. Vee asked,

"What time can we close?"

"Well, we can close when we like but I think we should stay open until about 10pm. Please pass this on to Prem and Lek."

As evening progressed the restaurant became busier. There were lights to be switched on in the garden and tables to be laid. Orn gave her assistance with this. Rob made some extra menus. Gradually they worked their way toward the end of their first business day. Rob arranged with Jira to go to a print shop tomorrow to get 200 menus printed. He gave Jira 5,000, saying,

"Bring me the change." At nearly 10pm the last customers left. Prem was clearing up his kitchen, Vee was checking the till.

Not long after this, the restaurant was closed and everyone went. SooSoo and Jira, hand in hand. Tarrin and Orn, hand in hand. Rob and Vee said goodbye to all the others as they climbed into a taxi. They were soon back at the Royal Cliff beach Hotel.

"We're in business!" was the last thing Rob said as he got into bed. Vee too, was soon fast asleep.

TAN and FAR

Among the new influx of customers who, as days went by, seemed to flock to, the new, 'Rob & Vee's', was a group of students from a nearby University. They were fast-talking lively girls who seemed to enjoy the food placed before them. They started to come at about 4.30pm every day. Then it was Tan, who happened to serve them. The result of this, was that he and a certain one of these girls noticed each other. The other girls urged her, to talk to him. "Hi! You seem to be making quite a habit of this place. I hope you like it," he said to the most appealing one.

"Sure – Are you the one who cooked it?"

"I do cook sometimes but I didn't cook today. As you may know, we are planning to expand so we are going crazy trying to find new staff."

"How do you keep alive? – I mean job?"

"I'm a pharmacist. I work at a pharmacy in Silom, called 'Silver Cross."

"Like the job?"

"Not much."

"Much easier working here, I should think."

"Or really?"

Tan's free day involved visiting a certain pharmacy. He arrived wearing his usual garb of slightly baggy trousers and shirt with rolled up sleeves. His mop of hair always looked unkept. She faced him across the counter, with white coat and a thermometer in the pocket.

"Sorry, I cannot talk to you here, but I finish at 4 pm today – Could you come here then and we can go somewhere together?" She was doing her best not to sound unfriendly.

"Sure, ok see you at 4 o'clock," Tan replied.

He certainly didn't want to make any trouble for her. Tan thought about what to do with her. He decided to just walk along the seafront with her and take it from there.

Far was nervous about getting too involved with Tan.

He seemed, in his casual way, to be a nice enough man, but she had not forgotten, a farang named, Jeff. She had been in love with Jeff. He seemed so sophisticated and always so confident with women. She was quite under his spell – just expecting and ready for some sort of sexual advance, when his phone rang. His conversation was difficult for Far to follow in detail, but it was full of "Dear" "Sweetie" "My Love"- as soon as it had finished, he collected his things saying,

"This is where I have to say 'good-bye,' – ok?"

She was aghast – Far didn't know what to say. He closed the door forcefully and she collapsed in tears. She was angry. Of course it was not 'ok!' She phoned him again the next day and put on her best act of boldness and courage. He made a date with her. She went to the place, where he said he would meet her, and waited, but he just didn't come. Far's little voice said, 'Well, he stood you up, wouldn't you expect him to do that?' 'Why didn't he come to you?' She had a whole list of answers and they were all painful. Far knew, she had to avoid any man like Jeff. Now in her late twenties, she thought, a plain girl like her, was fast running out of chances, to find a man to share life with.

Tan had a lazy morning and then waited for the magic hour to arrive. At 3.30 he started the trip to the pharmacy where she worked. He waited on the corner, where he could see anyone who went in or out. Various people came and went. 4 pm came – and went too. Suddenly, she emerged. She looked much more human, without her white coat, but her skirt and blouse were quite formal. Tan went up to her.

"Or, hello, did you wait a long time?"

"No, I just got here. How was your day?"

"All right, but I am becoming disillusioned with it."

"Why?"

"Well, it's 90% just selling pills from drug companies. It's my suspicion that these pills don't actually cure anybody and most of them have side-effects."

"So you have a pretty low opinion of the job you were educated to do."

"Correct, but sometimes we forget what education really is about. – It doesn't have to come from Universities!"

"May be you should be a journalist and get paid for expressing your strong opinions forcefully."

"And what about you, you work in a restaurant – what's it called?"

"Rob & Vee's"

"Do you like doing that?"

"Yes, I enjoy it, because it's a family business. I have learned a lot about cooking and management, since starting to work there. Also the people there are a good friendly crowd, so easy to work with."

"Sounds like you love your job?"

"Well, if anyone took it away, I don't know what I would do."

"Do you mind if I give it a try?"

"Not at all. We are always looking for more employees, because we are planning on expansion."

"And how often do I get paid?"

"Monthly – that's your share of the profits and your share of the tips. Last month I was paid just over 7,000 Baht."

"That sounds pretty good! – Well this is all about business. – Do you like me?" "Yes. You seem to me to be very intelligent, rational and organized."

"But not sexy – that's what you mean, isn't it?"

"Who says you have to be sexy? I didn't say that – what about you? Do you think I am sexy?" At this she smiled and said,

"I think you could be."

"Thank you. Where do you live?" They stopped walking and sat on two chairs. "In an apartment in a Soi just off Third Road."

"Wow, I have a place in Thappraya Road very near to Third Road."

"Can you show me where you live? You can tell a lot from lion's dens, you know."

"Yes ok – we'll just get a pickup truck." When they arrived, Tan paid for both and they walked to his apartment.

. . . .

"I warn you. It's a bit of a mess." Tan found a CD and put it on to play. Far sat on the bed. She had left her bag on the chair. She took off her shoes and lay back on the bed. The air conditioner was on. She loosened some of her clothing.

"I could just lie here all night and go to sleep."

"Ok, I can sleep on the floor, I suppose."

"I'm only joking." Tan flopped down next to her and looked into her eyes. They were two eyes full of hope and expectation.

"I want you to know that you can come here any time we both have free time. Plus, let me know, when you are ready to come to work with me."

"I'll come on Friday – if you can get that day off."

"Ok." They exchanged mobile numbers and Far said 'Good-bye.' The next thing Far did was to call the pharmacy to say she could not come to work as she wasn't well. She then went home, by metro, to her mother at Ramkamghaeng. Father was at work.

"Or, Far, darling, what brings you home at this hour?" (it was early morning and Father had just gone.)

"I have to talk to you and it's very important." Far's mother was unconventional, but well dressed. She was naturally artistic and creative. Beside her, Far looked plain, drab and slightly mousey.

"Well – what is it?"

"I am leaving the pharmacy."

"You are what? – Are you out of your mind?"

"But I have found…" Far began, attempting to explain why she was leaving, but was interrupted.

"Now, you listen to me, my girl. Your father and I have

87

worked and saved hard so that you could go to University when you left school. When you became a pharmacist, we were pleased for you, because it was the job for which you had qualified. Don't throw this opportunity away – What a way to show respect for what your parents have done for you!"

"Mother, I know that you and father have done your best for me. I will never forget that, but I have learned, that working in a pharmacy, is just selling people pills and potions, from pharmaceutical companies – These usually, have a calming effect, but do not cure any ailments. The problem is, that in most cases they have unpleasant side-effects. I don't want to spend my life, working for a pittance, dishing things like this, out to people."

"You have a better job than your Father or me, that's for sure. I think you are just ungrateful. It's not true you work for a pittance. You just want more and more – that's greed!"

"Yes, I want to be paid more, because I think I am worth more. I have met a young man who told me, I could work as he does, in a restaurant. It's much better money and he says they are all friendly."

"Here you go, chasing a rainbow. The same old formula – work for us! – All friendly – one big happy family! – And bags and bags of money. Did you know, your father went for a job like this and he nearly lost all his savings? Darling, don't do this. It's what they call, a 'scam.' It's too good to be true!"

"I will talk to my friend again, about it. But I will, definitely, not continue, being a pharmacist – I know the pharmacy is not a scam, but it's not the kind of job I want."

Friday came and Tan had managed to get the day off. At 8 am his phone rang, "Tan, is that you?"

"Hi Far, yes, it is me."

"I am in a pickup truck just outside your place and if you come here now, we can go to my apartment."

"Give me 10 minutes."

Tan checked that he was totally ready, then left his

apartment. Far waved to him. He got in the pickup and they went to Far's apartment. This time Far paid for the pickup and entered her apartment. Tan followed. Its exterior was, almost identical to Tan's Apartment, but the interior was immaculate.

"I feel cleaner, just entering this place. You have made it beautiful. I admire your artistic skill, in the way you have decorated it."

"It would not have been possible without my mum. It was all designed and decorated by her."

In any direction a photograph could be taken for a home-fashion magazine. "Would you like a cold drink – juice, iced coffee or coconut? Tan chose iced coffee and Far chose the same.

"Tan, I have to talk to you."

"Sure, what is it?"

"I spoke with my mother about the restaurant job and she said it was a scam."

"Really?"

"She is very bitter about my giving up the job at the pharmacy, because she and my father worked so hard to make it possible for me."

"I understand – perhaps I should talk to them – what do you think?"

"Could you come this afternoon?"

"Ok."

Far put on some music.

"Do you dance?"

Tan held her and moved with the music. He was not a particularly gifted dancer, but he had to go with what ever turned this woman on. She closed her eyes and held him close.

There then came a Samba piece and they both improvised and became quite excited by it. The beat was clearly marked out, by the words,

"Down in Rio, they do the Samba…" They both lost themselves, getting carried away, by this lively rhythm. But, Tan was waiting for the next 'hold me close' number.

It came and he held her again. This time she offered a kiss.

"Well, where would you like lunch? – a regular Thai restaurant or the 'scam' place?"

"Or, you mean, Rob & Vee's?"

"Yes, that's right."

"Ok" They took a taxi and were soon at the restaurant. Tan and Far, as regular visitors, on his off-day, were greeted and welcomed, as usual. He was asked: "Is she your girlfriend now?"

"When is she coming to work here?" Tan gave brief answers to these enquiries.   "I have an idea. I'll call my mother and invite her to lunch here – ok?"

"Brilliant!" Far, phoned her mother, giving her the name and address of the restaurant. Her mother agreed to come.

They waited.

"Another guest is due to come," they explained. SooSoo saw what was going on. She went to Far, for a quiet word. Far told her the whole story. This little story soon spread like wildfire among the staff. It reached Prem, in the kitchen. Everybody knew, this visitor was to be impressed! They waited for this famous arrival.

…………………………

"Good morning Mam! A colourful kaftan swooped in. Would you like to sit downstairs or upstairs?" Lek asked. She sat downstairs. Some music started. Orn came to her, to take her order. She returned to the table with some mineral water and a glass.

"Excuse me dear, you work here a long time?"

"No, I start 2 weeks ago."

"You like this job?"

"Yes, I love it."

"Thank you, dear."

The food arrived for Far's mother and she began to eat.

"Is everything all right Mam?" Lek asked.

"Yes, thank you."

As soon as her plate was cleared, a member of staff was ready to take it away.

"Excuse me, Mam, I am Tan, your daughter's boyfriend. She came here because I asked her to, so please don't blame her. I was responsible for her move."

"What desserts do you have?" Tan brought the dessert menu. She made a choice and he went to get it. When Tan returned and placed the dessert in front of her, she said,

"Do you love my daughter?"

"Yes, Mam, I do."

"I want you to know that I accept my daughter's employment here."

"Thank you mam. I will tell her now!"

As this lady continued to enjoy her dessert, a young woman rushed up to her, embraced her and kissed her cheek. Far was liberated by her mother's decision and felt enormous relief.

Far's mother was determined to finish her delicious dessert. She then ordered a coffee and, then left.

"Ok," she told Tan, "I start on Friday after I have said 'good-bye' to the pharmacy.

Tan and Far then sat down to decide what to order. It was an opportunity to enjoy their food in an atmosphere of relaxation. The music helped them. Far was beginning to warm towards Tan, who seemed to be always kind and sensitive to her. She had begun to think that to find a man like Tan would be impossible, yet here he was – she had found him!

"Is your food ok?"

"Yes, it must be, because I was so hungry," she said, smiling.

"I am sorry you had to wait so long."

"It wasn't your fault, but thank you for thinking of me."

"Can we go to your place?"

"Of course." They continued the business of eating and began to feel much better. They then paid their bill and took a taxi to Far's apartment. Tan sensed that 'this fruit was ripe for picking.'

"Can I take a shower here?" he asked.

"Yes, ok." He came out in his undershorts and got into the bed. Far took a shower and then reappeared in her bra and panties. She moved in with him and they kissed and cuddled. They spent some time looking eyes to eyes. They both seemed to share more of each other now. Far was a virgin, but she felt that at least Tan would be gentle with her. So she said,

"This is my first time like this,"

"Ok don't worry. No problem." Tan didn't expect Far to say that, but he was pleased in a way. He thought about his sister and what she had told him about the Laws in the Bible. He knew that love was supposed to come before sex.

'Oh God, I will have to tell her I can't do this?'

"Ok, my love, I am truly sorry about this - we have to talk."

"What? What's wrong?" The thought that worried Far, was 'Is this Jeff, all over again|?' But, at least, he had apologised!

"Nothing is wrong. Let's get dressed. I want you to know that I am stopping now because I love you so much."

"Well, I love you too, so what's the problem?" There is something more important than my love for you."

"Really?"

"Yes, my love for Jesus Christ."

"You know my sister, Vee, is Christian. I want to be Christian too. That means we follow Christian Law and get married first (if you agree) THEN have a honeymoon, - that's the word for sex."

"Is this your idea of a romantic proposal?"

"Well, I did suggest the question – it was, Will you marry me?"

"Are you sure you love me?"

"Yes and Yes."

"You love me *and* you will marry me?"

"Ok." Tan and Far now had a better understanding together. They were now fully dressed

"What's this Christian business – I'm curious?"

"I think you'd better ask Vee about that – I am just starting to learn about it myself."

"Ok, thanks – let's get a place together – may be a condo, ok?"

"I'm happy, if you are. I go to work tomorrow. You come on Friday. When we get a day off, together, we find a condo."

"Ok, I go now."

"No we can't do that, Far replied, "You stay here and go to work from here in the morning."

"All right, if that's what you want. Then I can tell you I love you." So Tan and Far freshened themselves, then settled down, to spend the night together. They held hands and in the darkness, consciousness slipped away.

In morning light, they, both awoke. He began to get ready. Far wanted to get him some breakfast. She searched in the fridge and her kitchen.

"Don't worry, darling, I'll get something on the way."

"Ok my love I just don't want you to be hungry." They hugged. They kissed and Tan went. He got a taxi to 'Rob & Vee's.' Near there, he went to a place to get his breakfast. He thought about Far and wondered what she was doing – probably getting ready to go back to the pharmacy, for the last few days. He called her. "Hi! Where are you?"

"I'm on my way to the pharmacy for just the last few days."

"Did you have a good breakfast?"

"Yes thank you, I have just finished it and I've just left home. See you soon, my love. Take care. Bye!" He paid the breakfast bill.

BUSINESS IN-SITU - 2

In Suite 42 in the Royal Cliff Beach Hotel, the morning alarm rang. Rob and Vee, both, woke up. It was time to shower and generally get ready. She remembered Rob's medicine and thought about getting more. A call to the doctor was all that was needed. She phoned and he said he would bring it. She transferred the brooch to the sari she was wearing. They had a short breakfast, down in the foyer, followed by a coffee.

They then got into a limousine and started their trip. They arrived at 10 to 9. Rob opened the restaurant but left up the 'closed' sign.

"I think when they get started today, we'll be able to leave them at it." Vee was enormously relieved to hear Rob's words. She realised only too well that this routine was putting far too much strain on him. If he wasn't very careful, his health would suffer.

It was another busy morning at work, but at 11.30am Rob left and Vee remained on the till. Vee phoned Jira, to ask him to come in for the till. He said he would bring SooSoo. So when they arrived there was some talk in Thai and Vee left the 2 in her place.

"Where has Rob gone?" was the question on Vee's mind. Vee took a taxi to the Royal Cliff Beech hotel. She went to Rob's suite and he was there stretched out on the bed.

"Oh I thought it was the maid, sorry, I am a bit tired at the moment." The in-house phone rang. Vee picked it up.

"Dr Ramsong is here to see Mr Simmons."

"Ok, please send him up."

The doctor arrived with more medicine and Vee paid him.

"How is Mr Simmonds today?"

"Much better, I think." He looked at Rob, smiling at both of them, then left.

....

ROB DIES.

"Would you like some tea?"

"That's a good idea." Vee phoned room-service. While she was speaking there was a strange buzz on her phone. As soon as she put it down it started ringing.

"Hello, this is reception. Mr. Simmonds is asking if he might visit you."

Vee was overcome by a strange feeling, of embarrassment that she could not explain. She was also slightly confused. She knew exactly that Cary Simmonds was at reception. 'But I must stay with Rob, he needs to have his medicine' said her little voice. She suddenly realised what a good idea had been suggested,

"Yes - he's welcome to visit us, please give him my room number."

"Thank you Mam." She turned to Rob, who was semi-conscious.

"That was your brother, Cary. He's coming here to see you." Rob roused himself. There was a call at the door. A trolley was wheeled in. On it was Rob's tea and Vee's cappuccino. The tea maid was a portly woman in a pale blue overall.

"Put it on my bill please," Rob called out.

"Yes, Sir." As the Tea Maid left, a tall elegant man arrived.

"Come in," called Rob. Although he was tired he couldn't help noticing the amount of time that Cary and Vee spent looking at each other. As it had now cooled, she helped Rob with his tea and gave him his two spoonfuls of medicine.

"I must thank you for taking such good care of my brother."

"Oh, it is my pleasure." Rob sipped his tea.

"Do you mind if I have an iced coffee from your fridge?"

"Of course not. You are our special guest." Cary

opened it and took out his carton. Vee started to drink her cappuccino.

"So it seems we both like coffee."

"Yes that's true."

"I would say, the greater truth is that we have quite a lot in common."

Vee looked at Rob. He was dozing. She began to talk about the business Rob started. Vee explained how hard the first day was and the ordeal of this morning. Cary understood well, what a toll that must have taken, on his brother. Rob started to rouse himself. Vee went to help him. He got up to go to the bathroom.

"I think Rob will sleep now." Rob emerged from the bathroom and sat in an armchair.

"Rob and I are business partners – Has he told you all about it?"

"Yes, I think so. It sounds like extremely hard work."

"Yes, it is especially for Rob."

"Do you like music?"

"I like Pumpuang."

"No, I meant Western Classical Music?"

"I don't know." She suddenly noticed that Rob had closed his eyes

"I will take him back to bed later."

"Tell me about that Thai singer – who is it?"

"Oh, Pumpuang Duangsri. She died."

Vee then proceeded to tell Cary all about this singer and how she helped popularise Thai folk music. It occurred to her that Cary was very easy to talk to.

"I think I'd better move Rob to his bed now."

Vee got up and went to Rob. She touched his arm to rouse him. Nothing happened. She touched it again and the arm moved but only because she had pushed it. Suddenly Vee was seized by fear and panic –

"ROB!!" she called out, almost screaming. He didn't move an inch. The eyes remained closed. Vee was distraught she drew a deep breath and collapsed in tears. Cary's arm was round her.

"I knew this was going to happen and I just let it happen – I let him DIE – that's what I did!" she shouted at Cary through her tears.

"You loved him, didn't you?"

"How did you know that?"

"I could tell by your reaction." Cary himself was quite sad that his dear brother had left this world.

"We had better report this to someone." Cary phoned and asked to speak to the Manager. He reported what had happened. Cary was himself near to tears. There was a sharp knock on the door. Two men entered with a stretcher. Rob's body was lain on it and taken from the room. It would need only one doctor to pronounce him dead and he would be taken straight to the farang cemetery in Bangkok.

Vee opened Rob's case. She was searching for something. In one pocket she found it – His Will. It would have to be sent to his Solicitor. She then found his list of phone numbers. Vee called everyone, to tell them the restaurant would not open today or tomorrow.

"Please tell me if there is anything I can do."

"See if there is anything else we need in that bag."

CARY and VEE Intro.

"All right, but Vee, you don't want to spend a night in this room alone – why don't you come up and share my room? – I am very easy going." Vee went around collecting all her things and Rob's. Then they left. Cary's room was bright and breezy from the air conditioning. He had a CD player and TV. Vee dumped her luggage on his bed and left Rob's things on the floor. Cary drew her towards him. They stood looking eyes to eyes, allowing a myriad of thoughts to pass back and forth. At the same moment, they both drew closer and kissed. There was urgency and hunger from both of them.

"Cary, my darling, can you do something for me?"

"Just say the word and I'll do anything you want."

"Well, can you take over from your brother and work with me, at the restaurant?"

"Yes ok, but that doesn't sound very romantic. Isn't there something else you want?"

"Yes, I'm hungry."

The truth of the matter, was that Vee, who had spoken so often with Rob about sex, found that now, that sex was available imminently, it terrified her – but she really was, very hungry. Cary went with her, down to the restaurant on the ground floor and they entered. This was a new experience of farang food, for Vee. It was delicious food – then a trolley came round with desserts. Cary chose Rum Baba and Vee chose Sherry Trifle. Coffees followed.

"Are you comfortable now?"

"Cary, darling, that was delightful." They meandered nonchalantly back to their room. Clothes were loosened and removed. Cary put on a CD quietly then disappeared into the bathroom. Vee listened to the music as she removed her shoes. Cary appeared and Vee entered the bathroom. When Vee returned to the room Cary was on the bed.

"Cary, darling - I am not an idiot. I know what you

want. But I simply cannot do anything at the moment. Rob has just died and I don't think it would be right."

"Ok, I think I understand. Don't worry. I have lost a brother, you know." Vee could not believe herself. 'This man is too good to be true – but he is real! He is here!' They made preparations and went to bed, separately.

Cary was slightly puzzled by Vee. 'She was all that time with Rob and yet she behaved like a virgin.' They slept.

The sun between the curtains woke both of them. Cary had decided that he had some serious talking to do with Vee. He was not at all, as smitten with her, as he had been. He had a strong impression, he was being led on, just because his brother had died. He decided, that breakfast was as good a time as any, to have it out with her. They took their trays and went to sit.

"Well Vee, I have to do some blunt talking with you."

"Sure, no problem. Anything wrong my love?"

"You have come, very quickly, from loving Rob, to loving me."

"To be quite honest Cary, it has been easier for me having you here – it has saved me from continued sadness, mourning Rob."

"Yes, I think I understand. What I can't understand is that you spent all this time as Rob's lover and you seem scared of *me*."

"I spent what? – Who said to you that I was Rob's lover? Was that some gossip you picked up? – I can tell you, I was not your brother's lover! I know what 'lover' means – it means sex! And I did not do that with Rob – we had an agreement and understanding about it. It was a very special relationship."

"Oh, I'm so sorry, I jumped to the wrong conclusion. It was foolish of me. I don't wish in any way to undermine your memory of Rob, or the special relationship you had with him."

"These mushrooms are nice."

"Yes they are – and I would like you to know, that I

love you now, more than ever – I mean. Vee, darling, I know you are a virgin. Don't worry about it." Vee started choking on her food. Cary handed her an extra serviette.

"Why don't you find a girl with more experience? I am not good enough for you." She said, hurrying off in a huff. Cary walked calmly back to the room. She came from the bathroom. He held her hands and looked into her eyes.

"Let's sit down. – I have never thought of you, comparatively, with other women. If you ask me to think of all my life and choose just one woman, who would I choose?"

"Your wife I suppose."

"I didn't know you then. I said if I could choose, from the *whole* of my life, any one woman, who would it be? – I'll tell you – You, my love – you are more to me than any other woman has ever been. I am so lucky to have met you."

"But I have no experience of sex. You know that now – aren't you disappointed?"

"Disappointed? What for? I can show you that stuff. It's nothing complicated. I am not showing you a music score and asking you to sing it – *That*'s difficult! But sex? – it's the same as the birds and the bees – what I mean is, it's quite natural"

"Like going to the toilet and 'tam kee?' (have a poo?)"

"Yes, like that, but with no bad smell." Vee laughed. She was glad she could talk, so easily to Cary, about everything and anything. She had loved Rob but, Cary was quite different. Not only younger and very good looking. He seemed always to know what to say and how to say it, so what did he see in her?

"Cary,"

"Yes, my love?"

"Why do you love me? I mean, I'm just a simple country girl and I don't know what you see in me."

"Country, yes. Simple, no. What do I see in you? Wow you certainly know how to ask big questions! – Well, I could come out with some platitudes, like –'I've always admired my brother's taste in women.' Or – 'I am at a turning point in my life, and you fit in to it, neatly.' What I must say is, you have taken me by surprise. I had no idea that I would find a young woman as attractive and interesting as you. I have never been, as excited with a woman, as I am with you."

"What about your wife?"

"Oh, you know about Rosita? She was stunningly beautiful. I loved her very much. Then, one day, all the beauty drained out of her and I saw the real Rosita. She fought a losing battle."

"I'm sorry, Cary, that must have been very sad for you."

"Yes, it was. But, Rosita was the sort of girl who wanted me to enjoy my life. As she lay dying, she begged me to go out and have fun, so intense was her love for *me*. But I couldn't go, of course. I stood by my Rosita, guarding her departure from this world." There were tears in Cary's eyes. It was the first time Vee had seen this reaction in him. She put her arm around him.

"You are very precious – you have a good heart."

He reacted by taking her in a deep hug. They spent a special moment in the comfort of each other's arms.

CARY and VEE - Debussy

"So, when *are* you going to go out and start enjoying your life?"

"We had better go now, my love, because tomorrow you want me to start work."

"Well, what can we do?"

"You could come to a concert with me and see how you like it."

"What concert, where?"

"An old friend of mine, will be playing the piano, in the Theatre in Pattaya. The programme is a series of Debussy Preludes – I recommend it to you."

"Well, let's do it, then. I've no idea what to expect but, if you recommend it, it must be good."

"Thank you, but first I must call at the Police Station, with my passport, to get my residency stamp." They took the limousine. Cary took only 20 minutes at the Police Station. They then continued.

"I think we are a bit early, but we'd better go in to get good seats."

They found places to sit near the front, just to the right of the piano. Cary wanted Vee to be able to see the pianist's face as she played. The pianist arrived, to a crescendo of applause. She was of light build and of an age suggesting a mother or aunt, perhaps both, but with a liveliness in her eyes. She got herself comfortable on her stool. A hush descended. Unobtrusively, she started to play. As the themes formed patterns and the music followed a description, it generated feelings in Vee that she had never had before and didn't know existed. The expressions on the pianist's face, communicated with her instantly. She was enthralled with the sound mixtures and patterns that came to her. Each prelude was a new adventure in sound experience. Cary was delighted to find, that Vee appreciated this type of impressionistic music. They reached a point at which a break was given.

It was a chance, for everyone, to stretch their legs and Cary was able to introduce Vee to a few of his old musical acquaintances. As they were speaking, suddenly, the gong began sounding, for people to return to their seats. There was a hush, then, even greater applause, as the pianist made her re-entrance. They all waited, in anticipation and the music suddenly, exploded with vigour and then developed, as a speaker would, when telling a story. But again, Vee found herself hearing something, for which there were no words. There were several more pieces, each one unique and a special delight to Vee and no doubt, many others in the audience. Cary spent this time in his own quiet world. He knew what to expect but he also knew he loved it. All too soon, it was time to go.

"I have never done anything like that in my life!"

"Well, there are often concerts, you just have to check the newspapers."

"Do I have to? I'll have you, to tell me what's on and where."

They were holding hands and swinging arms.

"Yes, my love, that's quite true, I was forgetting. I'll never need to be alone at a concert, now I have my Vee."

"Yes that's right, I'll always come with you, so long as you recommend it."

"Where's that taxi?" Cary waved and a taxi pulled up. They were soon back at the Royal Cliff Beach Hotel.

"Oh idiot I am"

"Why?"

"Because instead of lolling about at a concert, I should have done something about getting a condo for us. We can't live in a hotel for ever, but we are stuck here, all the while we are working."

"You can take a morning or afternoon off, because you're the boss." Cary immediately planted a kiss on her cheek.

"What would I do without you?"

"That's sweet of you to say, I think you would be very unhappy without me."

"Yes – may be even suicidal."

"Ok, understand but don't joke about that."

"Yes, sorry."

"I'm hungry"

"Me too." They went to the dining room and checked the menu. Having both worked up an appetite, they ate enthusiastically.

Back in the room they watched CNN on the TV. It was all about a typhoon in the USA. The time came for bathrooms and bed. They were both tired.

CARY and VEE – work -1

The alarm rang and a new working day started. Vee was confident that Cary would take over Rob's role as boss, even though he had not yet met his team of workers. After breakfast, Vee took Rob's Restaurant Book and gave it to Cary. He glanced over the papers quickly and thanked her. They arrived at the restaurant and Lek and Prem were already waiting by the door. Cary introduced himself and opened up. Soon, others arrived and it was time for work to start.

"Oh SooSoo and Jira, good to see you, my name is Cary. Rob was my brother."

"We are so sorry he died."

"Thank you. By the way, you two are off today. See you tomorrow, ok?"

"Ok Sir, thank you, but this is for you," Jira said, handing him a package and the change.

"Oh the menus – good of you to bring them on your day off."

Everyone else seemed to know what to do. Vee was on the till. Prem laboured in the kitchen and Tan shared the work load with him. Tan mentioned to Cary, that his sister, Noon, was interested in joining the staff.

"Just bring her along!" was Cary's reply. Tarrin came to him to introduce Orn, as a new employee. Cary received her politely.

"It's always good to see a new face here!" He received a shopping list from Prem, as expected. He took a taxi to the Central shopping mall and filled his basket with the items needed and any others he thought might be useful.

....

When Cary returned the restaurant was thriving. There was a menu on every table and it was about 50% full. Lek had put Tarrin upstairs to take orders and *he* was very busy on the ground floor. Prem was pleased with his new supplies. It all seemed to be ticking over nicely. Suddenly a farang woman was standing up and calling for water. Lek immediately took her a glass. She complained that the food was too hot and she had asked for 'not hot.' Cary went to her and apologized, removing her food and agreeing to provide her with another 'pad thai' with absolutely no chilli. When Cary took it to the kitchen he said,

"Ok bin this and do a pad Thai without chilli." Prem gave him a look and set to work.

"Where's my food?" the farang woman called out.

"Coming Madame, in just a minute or two, I promise you." Moments later. Cary was able to take Prem's creation to her table.

"Here you are Mam. I hope you enjoy it." Work settled back to normal. Cary began familiarizing himself with the menu. Meanwhile Lek and Tarrin rushed back and forth busily taking orders and serving.

"I can still taste chilli in it!" came the angry shout.

"I am so sorry Madame. Of course we will not charge you." She got up and left, having eaten about half the portion.

"We cannot avoid them sometimes but I hope we don't get another one like that. It's bad for business," Cary told everyone. Work continued and Cary decided he would leave the restaurant with Vee in charge so that he could look for an apartment. Vee wished him good luck. She got Orn to work, helping her, on the cash till.

CARY and VEE – Condotel and Proposal

Cary took brochures from several companies and scrutinized the floor plans. He then called 3 and made appointments to be shown around. It was not as difficult as he had expected. He wanted a good view of the sea – so a top floor or at least high up. His taste was for en-suite bathrooms. He marveled at the well-equipped kitchens. Then he suddenly realised he had hit on what he really wanted – It was called a 'Condotel' The advantage of your own Condo with the convenience of hotel amenities downstairs, so, restaurant, pool, gym, hairdresser, coffee shop and various boutiques, were all downstairs in that brightly-lit, glitzy world known as 'hotel' One was no longer just a guest, but a VIP, as the owner of a piece of the real estate. Cary looked around the condo before him. It seemed to him to 'tick all the boxes.' He then arranged to complete formalities with his lawyer. He took documents from the condotel, in another taxi, to the law office. Next stop was his bank, where he made a transfer, as agreed. Then, next day, would go back to the condotel to collect his key-card.

The restaurant, when he returned, had tables and lights in the garden. Only a few tables remained free. Lek was busy here as well as inside. Vee reported very high takings.

"I have some good news too," Cary replied, causing her to smile. The evening was progressing. People queued at Vee's till, then left. All the while, people, some single, some couples and others in groups kept coming. Then suddenly, Cary announced.

"All right, I am going to put the closed sign on the door and make sure it opens only one way." Outside, people arrived and went away again. Cary decided to do something about the music – he didn't think a radio station was good enough. He decided to get a CD player and provide some of his own CD's.

Eventually, the last customer left and it was time to

107

clear up. Vee got the sweeper. Lek wiped tables. Prem and Tan washed pots, pans, plates, dishes and cutlery.

Cary checked the till takings, in a bag – everything, then the paying back of the float. He realised it would have to be paid into a business account as soon as possible. It was time to thank everyone for their efforts and lock up.

Cary and Vee returned to their Hotel.

"Do you know this may be our last night here?"

"Why may be?"

"Because I don't know if we'll be able to move tomorrow."

"Why not phone Lek and ask him to come in tomorrow and be on the till with Orn."

"That was smart thinking." Cary checked his phone list and called them. They both agreed when they heard it would count as overtime. So in relaxed mode. Cary and Vee prepared themselves for crash-out.

"What would I do without you to think for me?"

"What would I do without you to understand me?" In their tiredness, leaving unanswered questions, they said 'Good night.'

Next day, Cary and Vee were both in high spirits to be without interruption, in each other's company. They first had packing to do and after their last buffet breakfast, checked out.

"Where are we going?"

"To my new apartment. I hope you like it."

"Well it won't be as good as a hotel."

"Why not?"

"Because here we can go swimming, get our breakfast or lunch. We can also go shopping. But in an apartment you have to go out for all those things."

"Yes, you are quite right." Vee wondered why Cary was suddenly silent on the subject. 'Perhaps he was working out how to change his accommodation again.'

The taxi arrived at another hotel.

"You said an apartment, but this is a hotel – why did you lie to me?" As baggage was unloaded Cary paid and tipped the driver. Hotel workers came as they mounted the steps.

"I don't understand," Vee persisted as Cary went to check in.

"Welcome Mr. Simmonds," said the smiling receptionist,

"Here is your key-card – 21st floor sir," she reminded him. The number 72 was on the key-card. The lift whisked them up to floor 21 in just moments. They walked along the corridor and Cary inserted his key-card.

"This is my apartment – it's called a Condotel." It's my apartment with all the facilities and benefits of a hotel. I hope you like it. Just go in and look around. Vee did what she was told. Open-mouthed she toured the apartment. Cary approached her.

"I am sorry. Please forgive me for calling you a liar. I didn't know what a condotel was but I do now."

"You are forgiven, but I hope you know that I would never lie to you about anything."

"Me too."

"By the way, remind me to take my CD player and CD's to work tomorrow, please."

"Sure I will. I will do anything for you Cary. You only have to say" Cary took this as his cue.

"Ok, undress and lie on the bed."

"What?" Cary repeated. Vee proceeded to do as she was told. She lay naked on the bed, having kicked the sheet down below her feet. Cary also started to strip. He stopped when down to his undershorts. He took the sheet at her feet and pulled it up over her.

"You must be getting cold," he explained.

"Ok, I think we trust each other."

"Yes, well. What do you mean? – Please hurry up. I have to go to the bathroom."

"Ok go," he said, turning to switch on the CD player. Vee took some underclothes on her way to the bathroom. Some music started. Vee returned.

"I am warmer now."

"Ok come. I want to talk to you." They lay together in their underclothes, both covered in bed sheet.

"You are Thai, ok?"

"Yes, of course, don't tell me you have just noticed."

"No, of course I know, but that's just it." There was very quiet background music.

"What on earth are you talking about?"

"Well, how do you feel about becoming Mrs. Simmonds."

"You mean Mrs. Simmonds the 2nd?"

"Yes, all right,"

"Is this a proposal?"

"Yes, I want to know, Vee. Will you marry me and spend the rest of your life with me?"

"Yea."

"You will, really – definitely?"

"Yes – I said yes."

"And you will never change your mind about it?"

"Never."

"I will always love you – and you will always love me?"

"Always."

They both got up and started to dress.

"Well, congratulations – we're engaged!"

They both put the final touches to their dressing and appearance.

"Let's go to work and tell everyone!"

"Good idea." Cary grabbed his CD player and some CD's. They took a taxi to the restaurant.

CARY and VEE - WORK - 2

"By the way, I want to change the name of the restaurant 'Cary & Vee's.' I think would be more appropriate."

"Yes, I agree."

When they entered the restaurant they were immediately in the hubbub of working life going on all around them.

"Ladies and Gentlemen!" Cary shouted, above the commotion. Vee translated, phrase by phrase.

"I want you to know that the two founders of this restaurant, myself and Vee, are now engaged to be married." As soon as Vee had finished, huge applause broke out. Many of the customers stood, wished them good luck and shook Cary's hand.

A young boy came up to Vee.

"Are you going to be a mummy?"

"Yes, I will be, that's right."

"I think you'll be a very good mummy."

"Thank you dear." She kissed his cheek and he rushed back to his table.

Eventually, a calmer state was restored. Business went on everywhere as usual. Cary took the opportunity to install his CD player. He got it all plugged in successfully and put on one of his CD's. It immediately transformed the mood of the restaurant. SooSoo reported good takings at the till. Tan announced that from Monday, he would swap with Prem. Noon, Tan's sister came to shake hands with them. Everything was running well. Vee and Carry were able to leave.

"Tomorrow we'll change the restaurant name from 'Rob &Vee's' to ''Cary and Vees'.' We need a sign-writer and I have to go to a Solicitor anyway."

Cary and Vee returned to their condo.

They were both pleased that the restaurant was thriving

Next morning, as they entered the lounge, Vee asked whether they would have a Thai or Farang Wedding.

"Probably both – but Rob's Funeral is our first duty."

"Oh yes. Please forgive me, I was forgetting dear, Rob. His Funeral must be our priority."

With thoughts of Rob's affairs in mind, they took a taxi to the Solicitor's Office.

The Solicitor scrutinized Rob's papers and went through them mumbling to himself.

"First Mr. Robert Simmonds made a UK Will which you will have to investigate with a UK Solicitor. He left all money in his Thai Military Bank account and Bangkok Bank Account, to his – er, to Miss Viraporn Willapana. He is the joint owner of 'Rob and Vees' Restaurant, Pattaya South Road. His share of ownership passes to his brother Mr. Cary Simmonds. - Here are Mr. Rob Simmonds' Bank Cards," he said, as he removed them from an envelope. With a pair of scissors he cut each one in two and replaced the pieces in the envelope. It was replaced in his briefcase with the scissors. He said the Funeral in Bangkok would probably be at 3pm on 31st at the Charoen Krung Road Protestant Cemetery. He was thanked and paid.

Their next stop was a sign writer. They explained what they wanted. He said he would call at the restaurant tomorrow and give an estimate.

Cary took Vee to a meeting of Pattaya Vegetarians. There was a delightful pumpkin soup to start with. There were then various dishes to choose from – all freshly cooked and vegetarian creations. They met several other vegetarian people and there was an interesting talk on Vitamin B12 in the vegetarian diet. Vee had not realised that so many farangs were vegetarian. It was time to go. A taxi took them back to their condotel. Alarms were set and they were both soon horizontally unconscious.

The alarm rang. 'Showers, get ready-1. Breakfast, get ready- 2.' Cary took his briefcase. The taxi took them to work. He opened up - set the door as 'closed' and they went in. More arrived. Soon Tarrin and SooSoo were in circulation in the dining rooms. Jira was in the kitchen with Prem. Orn was with Lek on the cash till.

"By the way, we don't take credit cards or bank cards, but we are getting a machine to do that next week." Orn was with Lek, watching and learning so that she would be able to take over from him.

"And there will be wages on Friday." This produced a spate of cheering and clapping. Cary had kept a record of takings versus expenses so in a few days' time he would work out the wages for each employee.

The sign writer arrived and Cary showed him the sign that was already at the front. He explained what he wanted and was shown some samples of writing. He agreed a price with the sign writer. Work started with ladder and paint.

It was time for Lek to leave Orn to cope alone. He watched her. She seemed to be okay as one customer after another came to her.

Vee and Cary left the restaurant and took a taxi. Business was going well so they could treat themselves to lunch. They went to their hotel restaurant. Vee had Thai food. She chose 'Pak Ruam' and Cary had a stuffed pepper with brown rice. They had juices and it was quite pleasant to be among the quiet buzz of farang voices as they enjoyed their food.

"I think we'll have to get that machine in Bangkok." Cary then gave his attention to the accounts. He went to the shop downstairs to buy envelopes. When Cary returned he put wages for each of the employees in each envelope. He wrote the names on them. Finally, he handed one to Vee.

"That's yours." He then calculated the profit made. From this, new supplies would soon have to be bought. Vee's mother had been very generous, but supplies were starting to run out again.

"I must ask Prem for a list when we go there tomorrow."

Eventually the day's work was done and they retired to their apartment. Vee ordered some room-service and enjoyed a supper with Cary, then they prepared themselves for bed. They were both tired.

The clock was in action again, to start this morning.

They got ready and managed to take themselves down to breakfast. It was soon time to take brief cases and bags in a taxi and zoom off to the restaurant. They arrived and both looked up with pride at 'Cary & Vee's' – their new name plate. Cary opened and entered. Others soon arrived. Before long everyone was in place and doing their job. Lek took a broom to continue some sweeping from yesterday. Cary counted the tips. They were for about 10 days. In all there was 6,420 Baht so he added 917 Baht to each of his envelopes. He gave 917 Baht to Vee. Then he went round distributing pay envelopes, telling each one there was an extra 917 Baht in tips. It was then time for Cary and Vee to go, leaving SooSoo and Jira on the till. Everyone now looked more animated, perhaps the pay packets had something to do with it.

When he and Vee left, Cary asked in a bank where he could get a machine for accepting card payments. The bank gave him a business card. Cary and Vee got into another taxi and showed the driver the card. It was quite a complex journey. Eventually they stopped. Cary paid and went into the rather drab building. There he met a Thai man who was rather large and not at all drab. His face wore a huge smile and he asked why we had come to see him. Cary explained what he wanted and several machines were immediately shown to him.

"This one you have, because easy to use and good phone line link." Cary asked how much and they agreed on a price.

"All right this in your phone line and that one to the electricity – got it? Then key in your code"

"Yes, I think so. Thank you." They said good-bye to this good-natured man in his old drab office.

A taxi whisked them to the Bus Station at Ekkemai and Vee bought two tickets. This was a side of Pattaya life not normally seen by men like Cary. People waited patiently. There was Thai TV and many small shops sold fruit and crisps for the busses and bottles of water. All the while busses came and went. Fans rotated and flies explored. Now and then a fond embrace or simply a burst of emotional conversation – the rest, just waiting and meditating. The Pattaya bus came. Soon Cary and Vee were on board, ready for their trip.

THE MAD TEA PARTY

On arrival in Pattaya, they walked to the main road and picked up a taxi to take them to their condotel. When they arrived Cary paid and then took their luggage up to their room. He hurried back to Vee, in the foyer, saying,

"This is a late tea time!"

"Oh yes, all right!" They shared a pot of Darjeeling and asked for some cakes. A selection of assorted cakes on a circular cake stand were placed before them. There were, mille feuilles, chocolate éclair, rum baba, Danish pastry, opera, langue de chat, apple pie, cream horn and madeleine. Cary thought they had excelled themselves with this performance. Enough to keep himself and Vee, in fine fodder well after the teapot had expired. It was a tea-party to say the least, beyond their expectations.

"I think we deserve to enjoy ourselves after working so hard," was Vee's comment as she indulged.

"As Lewis Carrol knew, there is something insane about all tea parties – perhaps I am the Mad Hatter and you are Alice."

"Mai kojai – sorry I don't understand."

"Not worry. I will show you the DVD."

"Thank you." This party actually did come to an end and the two guests returned to their apartment.

No Sooner had doors closed than Vee's phone rang. It was her mother. A long conversation in Thai followed. Cary looked at the papers from his brother's Solicitor. It all seemed to be in order. He would have to go with Vee to her bank. The phone call came to a close.

"She asked where we were and if she could come over and talk to us."

"Tell her I'll get her a place to stay here tonight. When's she coming?"

"In about one and a half hours." Vee called her mother and told her to be prepared to stay overnight. They went down to the foyer to await her arrival. They sat and read magazines and newspapers. Suddenly a Thai voice was heard that Vee recognized immediately. She rushed up to her mother and they hugged. Vee told her she needed help organizing Rob's Funeral. Vee's mother's face looked sombre. She felt a willingness to give all the help she was able to. They went to the desk and Cary obtained a room for her. She looked very professional in her business suit and received a key-card.

Conversations then followed with Vee as translator.

"Well what can we do for you?"

"Perhaps you are forgetting that I am a sleeping partner. I found your place and I stocked the kitchen. That was my contribution."

"Yes, I am well aware of that and it's now time for you to receive your first pay packet." Cary opened his briefcase and handed it to her

"Everybody else has been paid, now."

"Thank you very much."

"Well, I really want a business report. How is it going?"

"Extremely well, at the moment. Everyone is working hard and learning their job and we seem to be rushed off our feet every day, as soon as that door has an open sign."

"That's fantastic. I was sure it would do well. Well it's very kind of you to listen to me so now, if you don't mind, I'll go to my room." Vee saw her mother out, chattering all the time.

"She's very tired now."

"What about you?"

"Not me. You?"

"The night is still young."

"Aray na?"

"It means there's still plenty of time – it's not late yet."

"Oh so the night gets old, does it?"

"Maybe, but I have never heard anyone say so – We are getting into the realms of poetry here."

"Oh, you mean like Sunthorn Phu?"

"Oh, yes, I've heard of him – That's right!"

Cary and Vee called the desk to ask if anyone could bring the DVD of Alice in Wonderland.

"Yes, Sir. Customer she leave in room. We bring now for you to borrow." Moments later, there was a knock at the door. Cary was handed the DVD. In only a short time, it was starting to play. Vee was enthralled. They watched the whole story

"So I am like Alice and you are the Mad Hatter?"

"Yes, that's right."

"I don't think you are mad. I wouldn't marry a mad man."

"Ok I was not serious. I think Lewis Carol was telling us there is a very fine line between 'madness' and 'sanity' and we can all be a little bit mad, when life becomes difficult. He also suggests that what we think of as smartness and respectability, may be seen by other eyes, as madness."

Vee thought for a while. These were new ideas to her and having seen the video, she could see what Cary meant.

"Well, I have a very sensible idea!"

"What?"

"Let's go to bed."

"Brilliant!" They both started to undress and prepared for a night of sleep. There were bathroom routines and very soon, two figures were together.

Vee was comfortable with Cary. He seemed to understand her. They held hands and hugged. They enjoyed being together. It suited Vee - and Cary didn't mind. Sleep took over.

CARY and VEE - WORK - 3

The next morning was start at work, as usual. However, at breakfast they met up again with Vee's mother. They enjoyed the breakfast fayre then sat in the larger chairs with their coffees. Cary's phone rang. His solicitor had set the funeral as at 3.30pm at the Charoen Krung Road Protestant Cemetery in Bangkok on the 31st of this month. Cary thanked him and announced to everybody. The agreement was that everyone would attend. Madame Deeee, excused herself, thanked Cary and left. It was time to go to work. When they reached 'Cary & Vees' the restaurant was open and three had arrived. Cary shut the door. Prem handed Cary a list of the supplies he required. He and Vee immediately left by taxi for the Central Shopping Mall on Second Road. Cary found all the items on Prem's list and added a few he thought might be useful. They then began their heavily laden return journey by taxi. Prem was delighted to have all his supplies and set to work immediately, helped by Tan. Tarrin said he was at present paying someone else to run his Muay Thai (Thai Boxing) School. It had started very slowly but business was now becoming stronger.

The first customers had arrived.

"Good morning Sir – Good morning Mam," said the smiling Vee.

Lek ushered them to a table and began to take their order. Cary and Vee, pleased to see that the business was running well, took their leave. Just as they were going, who should they run into but Madame Dee – herself? – at that moment, about to enter the restaurant!

"I very much hope it meets with your approval," Cary said and Vee translated. A huge smile spread over Madame Dee's face, as she looked at him. They parted. There was a small commotion, as Madame Dee entered. Vee and Cary took a taxi.

"Thank you my love. You are also my secretary. How

would I manage without you?"

"You would have no hope. Your life would be chaotic. You would have to employ an assistant."

"All right. I know you understand. But you don't have to rub it in!"

"Oh you mean like the cream for my face. Put it on at night to make a white mask, then go to sleep. In the morning I have a white face!"

"Yes you've got the idea. But you haven't got a white face!"

"That's because I don't rub it in."

"In this case – I would say, it doesn't matter." The driver was amused by the conversation going on in the back. Suddenly they were home. The taxi pulled in to the entrance. They stepped out and Cary paid.

"Let's go to the Royal Cliff Beach Hotel."

"Exactly what I was thinking!" They hailed another taxi and moved straight off.

"I think we'll be just in time for lunch."

"Me too." The taxi arrived. Carry paid and they got out.

"No luggage, Sir – Madame?"

"No thank you, not this time."

They instinctively moved towards one of the restaurants.

"This is a Japanese restaurant."

"I know. Do you like Japanese food?"

"I don't know. Shall we try?"

"Yes. Good idea." As they entered, the Thai waitresses bowed low, like Japanese people. They were handed menu cards and directed to seats. Cary was pleased Vee was a vegetarian but the poor girl was left without much choice.

"I suggest Miso soup with mixed vegetable and rice."

"Oh you vegetarian, yes?"

"Yes we are."

"No problem – I bring you the vegetarian Menu- ok?"

"Yes please. That sounds great."

They looked at it together and selected, Yaki Soba (fried noodles) with vegetables. And Gyoza (Vegetable

120

dumplings). They also ordered miso soup and tofu salad

The food arrived. It was an enjoyable adventure.

"What's that music playing? Cary asked, hearing a song in Japanese.

"Its name 'Chensagu Nomana,' Sir."

"Thank you. It's beautiful."

"Thank you Sir – You are welcome!"

There was tofu and a variety of vegetables. Rice and soy sauce seemed to go together well. They were offered a drink called Pocari, which replaces lost electrolytes. It was cool and fresh-tasting. To follow, they selected Coconut Ice-cream with Passion Fruit Sauce –

"It's called 'mochi'" but all they had to do was point at it and show that they both wanted it.

"Well this is better for you than those French cream cakes."

"Yes, but it's nice to have variety." It was a pleasant change from their usual fayre. Cary got the bill and paid. They said 'Good-bye' and 'Sayonara' amid bows and smiles.

They continued to stay at the hotel, if only to avail themselves of the delicious breakfast. Vee's phone rang. It was her mother to say that her lunch at 'Cary & Vee's' had been incredibly delicious. She had never imagined that in a Pattaya Street restaurant it would be possible to get cuisine to that high standard. Vee reported this as soon as the Thai call had finished.

"Here we are in the land of la la la. The Hotel that has everything and more."

"Do you get commission for saying that?"

"No, of course not, just enjoy it."

"Yes Sir." Vee flopped on the bed

CARY AND VEE - bathroom

"Ok we use our underclothes as pajamas – but we must be clean first."

They both stripped down then he led her to the bathroom. Vee had never been in a bathroom with a man before.

"Well just help yourself to everything as if I wasn't here."

"You mean I can have a pee?"

"All right – but I'm not going to ask your permission for myself."

When Vee had finished, she started hanging up her clothes. Cary now naked, relieved himself. Vee turned to look at him, then continued running the shower. Cary came to join her and they stood in the bath together. Vee's little voice said,

"All this has happened so suddenly." They were – two naked and wet bodies. Vee was surprised at how attractive he had become. It was now time for drying.

"Ok, Towel for you. - Towel for me. – With this towel I dry you. – With this towel you dry me. Ok na?" Vee started to dry Cary's body. She started with hair, then did face and neck.

"Ok now I do the same with you." Cary began slowly and carefully. She hanged her hair over the bath and he rubbed it.

"Ok now show me your face." He took a dry part of the towel and dried it. Then he dried her neck.

"Ok you dry me now," she started with his chest. "It's ok, just rub it." Then she did his arms, under arms and back.

"Ok my turn again with you."

At this point Cary found himself looking straight at her breasts.

"Ok I will dry you." He folded the towel and padded her gently so that the whole area was dried. He then dried her arms and under arms. He ran the towel back and forth across her back.

"Ok you want to continue this - you drying me and me drying you - or shall we now dry ourselves?"

"Ok, yes, we dry ourselves, now."

They swapped towels and finished off drying their more intimate parts and eventually drying their legs and feet.

"Do you mind if I watch?"

"No" Cary found that if he watched her, Vee immediately stopped the bit of drying she was doing. So he stopped watching her. They both got finished and back into their underclothes.

"You were magnificent!" Cary said as soon as Vee appeared in the bedroom.

"You were very good too Cary. You are so good to me." Vee couldn't express what she wanted. She realised, after today's shenanigans, that there was something irresistibly attractive about Cary. Cary had something and she wanted it – very much. She could not say exactly what it was, but she really wanted it!

THE FUNERAL OF ROB SIMMONDS

Next day, talk at breakfast was funeral preparations.

"What do you think you will wear, my love?"

"I'd like to wear my long black skirt but it's at home."

"You mean in your mother's house?"

"Yes."

"Let's pick it up as soon as we get to Bangkok."

Breakfast soon reached the coffee stage. It was their last chance to sit calmly taking stock of the busy day ahead. They took some casual clothes in a small case for afterwards. Their first taxi was to the restaurant.

As soon as they entered, it was clear that everyone was working hard. As usual, there was no shortage of customers. Cary gave out an announcement that he asked Vee to translate.

"Dear Customers, ladies and gentlemen, including colleagues and all who work here – I wish you all to know that this restaurant will close today at 2 pm and remain closed all day tomorrow. This is because of my brother's funeral. It was he who started this restaurant." Vee then spoke Thai. The level of conversation rose, but people still seemed to enjoy their food. Relaxing music was playing and this probably had the effect of keeping them calm.

"Ok what do you say, we go to Bangkok now?"

"Do you have all your funeral things?

"Clothing, yes. But I still have a speech to write, what about you?"

"Yes I'll be okay when I have my skirt." They took a taxi and Vee phoned her mother to tell her they were coming 'for the long black skirt,' they said together in Thai.

Eventually, they reached Bang Na. Madame Dee was waiting for them. She was holding up the skirt on two hooks – it had a plastic cover – and a pair of black shoes. They politely refused her invitation to 'tea and fruit,' and told their driver "Landmark Hotel, please."

Their first reaction to black clothes was to begin brushing. Cary's suit and Vee's skirt both needed attention.

"Darling, I am going to need some time to myself because I must write this speech. I don't want to do it tomorrow at the last minute."

Vee went down to some of the boutiques in search of black hats, then wandered into the bookshop. She was interested to learn something about famous composers. Cary sat at his 'desk' wondering how to begin.

As soon as he began to think about his brother, it didn't seem so difficult. He started,

"I'd like to thank you all for coming here today to remember my brother." Then he continued –

"Cornelius Robert Simmonds was born at a time when the UK was just turning to, wild music, flower power and drugs. Our parents favoured our new freedom but they were still ambitious for us. Rob and I attended the same Primary School. Rob made progress quicker than me. He passed his 11+ and went to Leicester University. Unlike me, he was fascinated by numbers and would spend hours working out how a theorem was developed. His first job was in Woolworths. He left this to do a course in Accountancy. This enabled him to work at the Abbey National Building Society. It was from the Abbey National that he got his City job, in London. This was the high point of his career and we were all very proud of him. He married Salina Mankowitz, a Jewish girl. Poor Salina became infected with Cancer. It spread to other parts of her body and she suffered terrible pain. As the doctors were unable to do anything, it got worse and she died.

Rob was deeply saddened. Then one day, through an old friend, George Russell, he heard that he could go to Thailand and have a wonderful life. Suffice it to say that dear Rob landed on his feet, as he met up with and was helped by, Miss Viraporn Willapana, to whom I am now engaged.

She is the greatest gift that my brother, Rob, has ever given. Such generosity is typical of Rob. I will always be grateful to him."

Vee had returned and was waiting patiently. Then he read to her.

"What do you think?"

"My love, I think you write very well. Your words come from your heart." "Wow, thank you!"

....

There was time to relax and think of themselves.

"It's lunch time!"

"Oh yes!" They made their way down to the coffee shop. Vee and Cary both had a slice of Vegetarian Pizza with side salad. They followed it with two cappuccinos.

"May be, Rob is telling us not to rush into a Wedding too quickly."

"Yes, I thought that too. There is no hurry for us. I'm not going to run away and as far as I know you are not going to either."

"Of course not, my love. I'll wait for you for as long as you want me to. So we have no problem."

The shiny steel example of Cary's logic was rather harsh for Vee. She was like a child with a chocolate cake, who was told, 'wait a few more days, then have it.'

'Suppose my appetite changes,' was the most worrying thought in Vee's mind. 'Anyway, I am not a machine to be switched off and on, at the touch of a button!' With this sobering thought, Vee managed a smile. She knew Cary understood her.

He knew, already, what she was uneasy about. As day faded, they returned to their bedroom. Cary put on a CD he had brought. Kicking off shoes, they both lay on the bed. They lay facing, each gazing into the eyes before them. The music seemed to help. Cary's eyes were very expressive and changed as the music changed. Vee's eyes were a mixture of child-like wonderment and sudden response to audio stimulus now and then. They both absorbed the alluring visions before them. A good hour

126

was passed in this way.

"You had better phone everyone to make sure they have full details about tomorrow." Vee began to make calls. There were some longer conversations.

"That was a good idea, because SooSoo and Jira didn't know what time it was, several had forgotten the address and my mum said she already knew." Cary and Vee watched some CNN and then prepared for bed. They fell asleep holding hands. As Cary turned during the night, his hand disengaged. When he turned back some hours later, his hand found hers again. It was a cool way to wake up.

"It's the Big Day today. Charoen Krung Road Cemetery at 3 pm."

"Yes, darling, I know." They got ready and went down to the buffet breakfast.

"Well, it's coming up to Loy Krathong – that is when you can make a wish and if you are lucky it will come true It's the most Romantic time in Thailand."

"Ok when is it?"

"Next week, I think."

"You have a romantic wish, do you?"

"Well, I can think of one."

"Ok, me too."

"Good, we'll do that then?"

"Yes, certainly!" Cappuccinos were very good.

Suddenly Cary said,

"What about the wake? We haven't told anyone and we haven't arranged anything." Cary went to have a word with the restaurant manager.

"Yes, about 4.30 tomorrow. About a dozen people."

They discussed food and drinks. Cary returned to Vee smiling.

"Ok phone them all again please and tell them there will be a wake afterwards, here at the Landmark Hotel."

"What is a wake?" Cary explained. Vee then obeyed. When the last call had been made they returned to their room. It was dressing up time. Vee helped Cary, giving him the final touches, a brush here, a hair-smoothing there.

Then he helped Vee with her final touches. He cut a piece of cotton from the hem of her skirt. He straightened her white blouse. Then he came to her face.

"Just a minute, these lips are a bit dry." He gave her a kiss.

"You're a naughty boy. You didn't do it properly,"

"Is your hair ok, up like that?" he asked, scrutinizing it.

"Oh, let me put your bow straight," Shoes were best black and shiny. Eventually both were ready. Mirrors were consulted. It was time for early lunch. It was just a snack between breakfast and wake. They went to the coffee shop feeling like Dracula and his bride. They both had a cheese croissant and a cappuccino. Cary took a further look at his speech. Vee examined herself in her vanity mirror.

They went back to the room. Carry explained to Vee that a priest would come and they would say prayers for Rob.

They were both ready. Cary had an old music case with his speech in it. Vee suddenly realised that she was about to do something for Rob – the last thing she could ever do for him. They took a taxi to Charoen Krung Road and entered the cemetery. There were several friends from the restaurant already there. There was a muttering of conversation in Thai. Cary thought that these proceedings probably looked quite strange to them. The hearse arrived, - a huge black shiny car, containing a coffin. Cary joined the men who would bear the coffin to its ordained place. Vee followed, with others behind her. The coffin was then hoisted and lifted down into the grave. The priest began prayers. Soon he was intoning the words familiar to Cary and all farangs,

"Ashes to ashes and dust to dust." Cary threw some earth on the coffin and Vee did the same. There were more prayers.

Cary stood among the people and began his speech.

From time to time he paused for Vee to translate. As Cary finished he made an announcement about the wake, which Vee immediately translated. The priest gave a blessing to everyone.

People began to go. Vee realised she had said good-bye to Rob for the last time. Cary stood by her and held her sobbing in his arms. His own eyes were watery.

"Come. The wake! We must go!"

"All right, my love." They took a taxi back to the Landmark Hotel. The Manager, good to his word, had made fine arrangements. There was a huge buffet, plus juices and some wine. It seemed that the entire staff of 'Cary & Vee's' were there celebrating, for the man who gave them a job and a future. The manager remembered Cary's request for music. So there was some music and dancing. SooSoo and Jira were well pleased and Cary held Vee as they moved about. Tarrin and Orn enjoyed themselves and Tan danced with Far. There was plenty of food, so everyone's appetite was satisfied.

"We are all very happy, right" This produced a wild cheer.

"Well, this is Rob's final gift to us. He wants us to be happy."

The wake went on and didn't finish until late in the evening. Only then did guests start to leave. Cary and Vee went to thank the Manager.

It was time to go back and change from these morbid clothes. In their room Cary and Vee were relieved to free themselves of these sombre accoutrements. There were showers and bright clean clothes with which to grace themselves.

"I don't know about you but I feel like some fresh air. Let's go down and sit outside."

"Good idea." So in the more relaxed mode of shorts and tee-shirts, Vee and Cary entered the outside world of the Landmark.

"Well I hope you like farang customs."

"What do you mean?"

"Well, you are due for another one soon, straight after Loy Krathong, or have you forgotten?"

"You speak about it as if I might not like it."

"Did I? I'm sorry."

"Can't you say what you are talking about or does it embarrass you?"

"All right, I'm talking about our wedding. It does embarrass me because you are so beautiful – if I was marrying a plain-looking woman I would not be embarrassed."

"So I am *not* plain-looking? – Can't you be honest?"

"Ok, I'll be honest. There is nothing plain about you. There is the unusual, sophisticated, exotic, original, unique and delightful – about you – but the idea of 'plain' is not related to you in any way."

"Yes maybe I am nice to talk to but I have a plain face."

"If you have a plain face, how come it occupied over an hour of my attention last night while we were listening to a CD?

"May be you have bad eyes."

"Well I can read a music score in a dimly-lit room."

"Ok"

"Well, you still want to marry me – or have you changed your mind? – but I want you to know I am marrying a beautiful girl. If you think you are letting me down, because you are not beautiful, then don't do it – don't marry me!"

"You ask me a lot of questions then tell me not to marry you. Don't you care?"

"Excuse me Sir, Mam, we want to close this part of the hotel now. You are welcome to come inside."

Cary and Vee thanked this uniformed man and stood up to go. They went back inside and then to their room

"Right, one question."

"Why?"

"What do you mean?"

"That's one question."

"No, I mean I want to ask you one question."

"Ok"

130

"Are you beautiful or not?"

"Ah so it worries you!"

"No, but it concerns me what you will say – so please answer."

"Not"

"You mean you are not beautiful."

"Yes – not."

"But if I don't agree with you and I say, 'you are beautiful,' shouldn't you respect my opinion?"

"Ok you think I am beautiful."

"Yes, that's it."

"So I let you down. And I have another problem."

"What's that?"

"I am crazy."

"No, you have a good mind and there is nothing crazy about you."

"You don't know."

"Ok you are secretly crazy." Vee allowed herself a smile.

"I am crazy about you – Cary Simmonds!" Her face reddened with embarrassment.

"And I am crazy about you, Vee." They got up from the chairs they were occupying. Vee went to the bathroom. Cary lay on the bed, having removed his sandals. Vee returned to him.

"You crazy about me?"

"Yes, I am."

"Ok, you ok, me ok"

"Yes, I think so."

Cary went to the bathroom. Vee was suddenly overcome by the idea that she had been giving Cary a hard time.

When he returned, Vee was in more amourous mode. She embraced him and they kissed.

"So we are going to have a Wedding then?"

"Ok one Thai Wedding and one Farang Wedding." Vee phoned her mum.

They began getting ready for bed. It reached the

moment when Cary was quite ready to go to sleep, but this conversation went on and on. Cary began to doze. Suddenly he was being shaken.

"My mum she organize Thai wedding ok?"

"It took all that time to say she would organize the Thai wedding?"

"No she agreed in just a few minutes."

"So why did you take so long?"

"Well, she's my mum!"

"Good night my love.

CARY AND VEE WEDDING PREP

Next morning it was time to check the restaurant. They were up early, for a quick breakfast, then off to Pattaya by taxi. The laundry at their Condotel would be very busy. They arrived at the restaurant with their baggage. The Restaurant was open and the expected staff were there, working hard as usual. Cary knew he would have to do the till and tips. He did the tips as the till was busy.

This time, it came to exactly 7,000 Baht, so there was 1,000 Baht for everyone. Cary took it home, to put the money in his envelopes.

On the way home, Vee said,

"I must buy you a silk shirt."

"Really? Why?"

"You need it for a Thai Wedding. It's our custom."

"Ok – I must buy you a wedding dress."

"A what

"A special dress that farang women wear, when they get married. It's white."

"Ok."

"Why are we having two Weddings, Thai and Farang?"

"Well, some will prefer one. Some will prefer the other. Maybe some people will come to both."

"Ok, I'll get the Thai one organized, and you get the Farang one organized."

"Ok" They were at home together, in their apartment in Pattaya. They left together by taxi. Cary asked the driver about a church. He said,

"Ok I take you Pattaya International Church. Priest is Hollander."

He and Vee went into the Church and spoke to the Dutch Vicar. Cary made an appointment for his wedding and reception at the Montien Hotel. He ordered that flowers would be put in the church and that somebody would provide him with a bouquet of orchids.

"You must invite my mother," Vee reminded him.

"Better that you do it." Vee then called her mum and they started nattering away in Thai. She changed to speaking a little more slowly and carefully.

"Ok she happy to come."

"Tell her Wednesday the 25th November." Vee spoke, then she replied to Vee. "She said it is a very good date for a wedding and she wants to come and try our food." Cary and Vee were therefore in good spirits, as they returned to the Condotel.

As they sat in the lounge, talk was of wedding arrangements. Cary mentioned a couple of churches he knew, then Vee said,

"But I am Buddhist." She was then asked to explain her idea of a wedding. – People being invited to a house – Blessings by monks. Rice being thrown,

"Just like SooSoo and Jira!"

Cary and Vee got a taxi to Pattaya bus station and then the bus for Bangkok. About two hours later they arrived at the Bus Station at Ekkemai. Cary decided the Emporium would be the best place to look. A taxi got them there, in just minutes. They took the lift and were very soon, in the department made for them. There was all kinds of Wedding apparel.

Vee picked out a few dresses

"Lorng doo, dai mai, ka?" she asked and disappeared into a cubicle with them.

Cary looked at this massive white figure. Vee turned right and left, but it was not quite her style. She went back to the cubicle. The next one was a sensation – It had been just made for Vee's figure. As she turned it swooped gracefully. There was even a net over her face, which she immediately raised.

"I think that's it – but let's see the other one." Vee went back and a while later reappeared with a new wedding dress. It was ok but they both agreed it was too old-fashioned.

"So that's it. We'll get this one," Cary said, holding up No. 2. Vee was delighted and very excited.

"Oh just one thing – these shoes are not quite right."

"I was just going to say." They asked the assistant.

"What about this style?" he asked producing a pair of 'Wedding shoes' Vee tried them on.

"No smaller, I think, I am size 6." The assistant took the shoes and disappeared. Moments later he reappeared, with a different pair.

"Yes, I think so," Vee said, standing up and starting to walk about.

Cary and Vee then left the department, well pleased with their acquisitions. "Where can I get a silk shirt?" Cary muttered to himself.

"Next floor up sir, men's shirts and suits," replied a helpful smiling assistant. Cary chose an ultramarine blue silk shirt. He tried it on and it felt comfortable.

"It suits you, Sir." The assistant said. Vee agreed. The next thing they did was to take themselves to one of the many restaurants. They were able to deposit their shopping bags for a small plastic disc. The food was Italian style. Pasta and salad. Time to return to Pattaya arrived.

They took a taxi. This gave them enough time to call at the restaurant. Cary asked for their apartment first so that he could pick up his envelopes and leave their luggage. They arrived just as the restaurant had closed. Cary entered with Vee and immediately checked the till. The takings, less the float, amounted to 9,930 Baht. So it was 1,418 to add to the 1,000 already in each envelope. Cary carefully made up each envelope. He then went around giving each worker their envelope. Last, came Vee's and his. Everyone was pleased to get paid again. Vee's phone rang. It was her mother asking about the Thai Wedding. She suggested 'tomorrow morning.' Vee asked Cary.

"Why not?" Vee continued to speak to her mother. She then said something in Thai to everyone present.

"What was that about?"

"I told them the restaurant would be closed tomorrow and the Wedding would be at a house in Bang Na."

"Good. You think of everything." Vee flashed Cary a smile. They went home to their apartment.

"Let's check Loy Krathong, this evening. You need to take a photo of me and a photo of you." Cary found the necessary photos.

"Ok" They took a taxi to a local lake. Vee spoke Thai with the driver. They bought a krathong, placed the photos in it, lit the candles and launched it. They watched their krathong make its way out across the lake. It seemed to be becalmed, then sailed on a little before stopping again.

"Ok, that's it, we will now have good luck." There were many other people doing the same thing. Cary and Vee left.

"Perhaps this is all that is left of my Buddhism," Vee remarked, in the taxi. They soon were home again and preparing for the night together.

CARY and VEE – THAI AND BRITISH WEDDING

Next day they started as usual with the hotel's breakfast. Cary then put on his silk shirt with his suit and Vee wore a dark green Sari. They took a taxi and after about an hour, arrived in Bang Na. They were slightly early but some people had already gathered outside the house. We waited for the monks to arrive. A shiny black car drew up and the monks poured out of it. They entered the house and began chanting. Vee and Cary were then ushered in and crowds followed them. When eventually the chanting stopped it was the signal for rice to be thrown at them and a gaggle of conversation to start.

"Congratulations you are now married," said Vee's mother in Thai. She translated for Cary. They both smiled and some photos were taken by professional-looking cameras. Others held up their mobiles for a shot. Cary learned that they were going to be in the local newspaper. The car with the monks drove away.

They and many of the guests then went to Madame Deeee's house for a gathering. Madame Deeee had put out a magnificent spread of snacks for the guests. There were also juices and wine. Various introductions were made. There was a queue of people to meet Vee. Cary met several people who spoke to him in struggling English. He tried to answer in friendly but plain simple terms that would be readily understood.

"You lucky man. Take good care Miss Vee, Yes?"

"Thank you. Yes I am very lucky. I will take good care of Vee, sure!" Then he was surprised as one after the other, the staff from 'Cary & Vee's' came to congratulate him, in almost fluent English. Although Cary was slightly out of it, not being able to natter in Thai, he enjoyed the atmosphere of animated and lively conversation, from people who were glad of a chance to meet each other again – and at the same time get some free food!

It was later in the afternoon, that they took themselves and an amulet that Vee's mother had given her, back to Pattaya.

They entered their apartment

"Well now we are married and we are not married!"

"Up to you!"

"I never realised how useful that expression was. Come here Mrs.!"

He held her in his arms and they kissed."

"I'm not Mrs. anything yet."

"I know but you will be soon – on Wednesday 25th November, in fact."

"That's next week."

"Yes, we'd better make sure we are ready for it."

Cary had to book the Montien Hotel for the reception and asked that the organist could play Mendelsohn's Wedding March. He still had to speak to the Priest about a man to give Vee away.

These matters were on his mind as they went down for their evening meal in their Hotel's restaurant. It helped to relax them.

"You have to tell me what to do, because I don't know anything about it."

"There is nothing to remember. A man will take your arm and lead you up the aisle of the church. That's the space in the middle between the seats."

"Yes, I know, but who – what man?"

"Normally it is your father. But as your father is no longer with us, it must be someone in his place."

"Who?"

"I don't know yet. The priest will know a man who will volunteer for the job."

"Ok"

The food was as good as ever and when they came to desserts they suddenly realised how good their life was and how fortunate they were, that everything was progressing so well.

Nothing on CNN or BBC could dampen their spirits, as

the time for sleep approached.

On the day, an early morning start was called for. Cary had now arranged everything. Vee's mother arrived and said she had her own room. She and Vee then left Cary to his bachelor isolation. Vee called him and said she would arrive with her mother. Cary would arrive alone. There were many guests starting to arrive. Cary met the priest and was introduced to that man who was going to give Vee away. He was friendly and able to speak some English. Cary went to his place in the front and the Church gradually filled.

....

The organist was playing quietly pleasant music, to bring out pleasant and relaxed feelings in everybody. Then suddenly the familiar introductory chords of Mendelsohn's Wedding March sounded. At the back of the Church, the smartly suited man Cary had met stood with the veiled Vee on his arm. Many heads turned as they proceeded slowly up the aisle to the accompaniment of the music. Vee was carrying a bouquet of orchids. She then left her escort and stood beside Cary. The priest stood before them and proceedings began. Cary's best man, Jira, appeared at his side in a very smart suit. At the appointed moment, Jira produced the ring, Cary had given him several days ago. Cary put it on Vee's finger. They repeated after the Priest,

"With this ring, I thee wed – With all my worldly goods, I thee endow…"

They each repeated as required and the words,

"I now pronounce you man and wife," were intoned. The congregation sang another hymn. There was a final prayer and blessing. At this point Cary and Vee were concerned that everyone knew that the reception would be at the Montien Hotel. It was a short trip and some people walked. Cary and Vee arrived like many others, by taxi. The Montien put on a grand display for them. They had obviously done receptions before. There was, at Cary's request, music, but it seemed that it was the food, that interested people most. Soon, everyone had some chosen morsel or huge slice on their paper plate, with a tissue. Vee's mother had produced a tiered Wedding Cake and it was cut for everyone to try. There were all sorts of fruits and Thai desserts in addition to cakes, meringues and brownies. It made quite a feast. All the guests enjoyed themselves. SooSoo was intrigued at all she saw, at this, her first experience of a farang wedding. Jira was also surprised, though did his best to fit in. As a result of his job, his English, like that of most employees of 'Cary & Vee's' had improved.

HONEYMOON

At a certain point, they made their exit, waving good-bye. A car was waiting to take them to Suvarnabhumi Airport. The secret destination they had both agreed upon, was India. They arrived in Chennai and booked in to the Taj Coromandel Hotel. It was a bit like a commercialized Krabi. The hotel food offered numerous options for vegetarians. They were naturally happy together, after all, this was actually, in reality, their honeymoon. Although, if the truth be known, Vee was both excited and terrified at the same time. This subject she had bantered about so often with Rob, dear Rob, with whom she had pretended to be so eager. Now all this bravado had gone. She was up to her neck in it and they were face to face. Actually, Cary had quite a kind face. Almost in a cloud-like existence, they let the day slip by, to late afternoon. It was only then, that they both seemed to gravitate towards the bedroom, as if it was an inescapable room of torture. First Cary put the 'Do Not Disturb' notice on the door. Then, he brought up the subject of 'lighting.'

"Shall we close the curtains? We don't want any passing birds to pry on us, do we?" Vee managed a laugh, but it was short-lived. Cary closed the curtains. The room was in semi-darkness.

"Like this or lights on?"

"No, no lights. Like this is fine."

They both set about the familiar business of undressing. Shoes – outer garments.

Cary moved to Vee and felt the soft curvature of her body. She enjoyed his presence because she knew he was gentle. He carefully removed her underclothes.

"Now you remove mine."

She came to him and began, fumbling with his undershorts. He helped her take them down. She then took his vest off. They stood before each other in their total nakedness. He led her to the bed. They came together in a hugging kiss. Vee found herself again with that feeling of wanting something from him. He enjoyed feeling her body and she explored his, tentatively. He rolled on top of her. They were still face to face. There was more kissing. He started going into her. His body tensed as he pushed. She winced at the painful sting. Suddenly, Vee realised this was something to be enjoyed, as they began to find a natural rhythm together. It seemed to her, to be reasonably good. What really pleased her was that, obviously, Cary enjoyed it. 'I must do this for him again,' her little voice said. However, Vee was the kind of girl to whom 'caution' and 'attention to detail' came as second nature. She began to wonder how much it might hurt the next time, as she stepped out of the shower, allowing Cary to go next.

"Wow that makes you hungry, doesn't it?"

"Oh yes, you are quite right. It's because you use a lot of energy."

They dressed and meandered down towards the restaurant.

"I would to thank you Vee. You're very brave."

"What? Why?"

"It was your first time and you gave a magnificent performance."

"Thank you but I am not a musician."

"You're better than that."

"Really?"

"To me you are."

"Thank you. That's very kind of you."

"Do you like this curry?"

"Yes green curry is one of my favourites. It's made with coconut, you know."

"Oh, why didn't I order that? Ok I will, next time."

"What's yours like?"

"Very good, I haven't had vegetable pulao for a long time."

"What are those things on the side of your plate?"

"They are the cases of cardamoms."

"Aroy, mai? (Does it taste good?)

"Aroy si," he replied, as the conversation became Thai.

Their desserts were also different. Cary had gulab jamons and Vee had a Thai dessert with coconut milk and ice.

"Can I try some of that?"

"Yes, help yourself."

She plunged her spoon into the jamon to take a piece and some of the spiced honey with it.

With his spoon Cary took from Vee, some of the various fruits and the liquid that went with them.

They were both very appreciative of each other's desserts as well as enjoying their own.

There were coffees to follow.

Cary asked for café au lait and Vee ordered the same.

They sat watching the TV in the lounge. They were showing a programme about St Thomas's Cathedral, in Chennai. It talked about the development of Christianity in India.

When it suddenly finished, they both realised how tired they were, so returned to their room. After Vee's session in the bathroom, Cary followed.

They were then together in bed, enjoying the coolness and feel of the body next to them. Both were too tired to do more than that.

Morning came with sun glaring through the curtains, but the room remained cool. They both got ready then dressed to go down to breakfast. The hotel put on an attractive buffet and obviously pandered to British tastes with, cornflakes, muesli, fried or scrambled eggs, toast and marmalade. There were also grilled tomatoes, mushrooms and sausages. For vegetarians like Vee and Cary there was hummus, tahini and a good selection of salads to choose from. They soon loaded their trays and returned to the table. There was water and various juices. It was quite a sumptuous breakfast. There were even beans on toast. They had missed nothing. Eventually they each had a small cappuccino. The TV in the lounge was still playing.

They were showing a DVD about India and its tourist spots. Cary and Vee gave it some attention, then made their way back to the room. It was a slow lazy morning and they both enjoyed the easy pace. Vee was first to disappear to the bathroom to freshen herself and cast of some clothes. As soon as she reappeared, Cary followed her example. They flopped together onto the bed and began to undress each other. Suddenly Cary leapt up and went to the door and opened it. He turned the notice to 'Do Not Disturb,' reclosed the door and rushed back to the bed. Moments later, they were both naked. They came together touching and feeling the body before them. Then Cary grabbed her and they began to kiss. Vee was waiting for Cary to finish kissing. He came on top of her, but supporting himself, as if he was approaching something very delicate. Then he pushed.

"Or!"

"Oh sorry does it hurt?"

"No, not now." Cary began to move and start a rhythm which Vee followed. It gathered energy and drew enthusiasm from both of them. Vee found herself approaching an experience of pure delight that she had never had before. Cary focused on his effect on her. He increased the pace and energy. Vee suddenly screamed and tensed her whole body. Cary held her in her ecstasy as he drove her even further. They then collapsed into kisses of gratitude and congratulation. They were hot and tender but totally obsessed with their task of pleasuring the other. Eventually they both lay exhausted and began to laugh at each other.

"You never told me it was like that,"

"Well, what was I supposed to say? You didn't tell me you were so good at this. You were like an expert."

"Really, was I?"

"Yes, I didn't expect much from you at all, but what did I find? – A sex bomb!" Vee started to laugh.

"You really think so?"

"Sure I do."

"You were very good too."

"Oh it was easy for me, just to do what comes naturally"

"Yes, but you were very nice to me."

"Yes, that's because I love you."

"Me too."

This mutually, self-congratulatory conversation, gradually wound down and the bathroom was again the destination of choice. When they were both clean and dry, Vee helped Cary to dress and Cary helped Vee to dress.

"Hey, misses, we go home tomorrow."

"Why you call me Misses?"

"Well, you are Mrs. Simonds now, that's all."

"Yes, I suppose so, but I don't like it much."

"Don't worry, to me you are 'my Vee' and you always will be."

"And you will always be 'my Cary'"

They left, changing the notice on the door. And returned to the lounge. It was time for some exploration. They left the hotel and began to walk in the hot air, along the sea-front. On the way they bought a coconut each, to drink and eat. It was a white beach with turquoise sea, not unlike parts of Thailand. They came to a bar. It was the point at which, to turn back. As they re-approached the hotel, they noticed in the distance, a number of boats. It was the famous Chennai Marina, but for Vee and Cary, who were now hot, it was time for the cool comfort of the Hotel again.

....

"Oh look it's another episode of Oshin! They have it here in India too!" They sat again facing the TV, for this absorbing story. It was now in English! However, they soon realized that this was the final episode. The middle-aged, Oshin was now the owner of a supermarket – the first shop of its kind in Japan. There were later, scenes of her son laying flowers on her grave. "Now we know what's coming!" Cary remarked. When it finished, it was time to find some rest again. They returned to their room, realising there would be no more Oshin in Chennai.

Well, this is our last evening in India. We should see the city before we go back to Thailand.

So they left the hotel again for the tropical night of India. They took a taxi downtown. The stalls were well-lit and enticing. The roads, quite chaotic. The taxi pulled over and stopped. Cary and Vee got out. He paid the driver.

They were entranced by the bustle of activity. There were strings of lights between the stalls. They walked on with light streaking the street. Then they reached the main road. There were several lanes of traffic in each direction, but the number of lanes, seemed to be in a state of flux. There was a cacophony of honking, beeping and hooting. Then gradually the traffic movement started. There seemed to be for most people a rule that, to make progress, it was necessary to change lane. This tended to create all sorts of jams, but somehow the traffic was starting to move. A rickshaw driver had stopped just near them.

"Where you go Sir?" he asked

"Taj Coromandel Hotel."

"Ok I take you." So Vee and Cary climbed up and the rickshaw began its sedate way back to the hotel. When he stopped, Cary and Vee climbed down and Cary paid him.

"Thank you Sir – thank you very much!" he said, seeing the money Cary had given him. They entered again the cool calmness of the Taj Coromandel Hotel. They went straight to their room. It was time for bed. With the usual preparations completed, they again found themselves side by side in bed, body to body. Holding hands, they slept.

It was a sober morning heralding their departure, but both of them were determined to start with sex. They just followed instincts automatically, both being now aware of how to read each other's body signals. It was an easy indulgent start to morning consciousness. There were cuddles and kisses, as a prelude to the mechanics, which followed. Gradually, a rhythm began to take shape and

146

slowly little by little, increase in pace. Vee became very excited and sounded extremely appreciative. Cary seemed to give a burst of energy driving Vee to ecstasy and causing himself to have a seizure. He was incapable of any further movement and Vee had reached her climax. There were some mutually congratulatory kisses and hugs, but it was getting hot and sticky.

Very soon they were obliged to leave the bed and head for the resources of the bathroom. Vee sat and used the bidet shower. Cary ran the bath tap to wash himself. They then both had showers and freshened up. It was time to dress and go for breakfast. Eventually they left the room together and went hand in hand to the restaurant.

It was their last breakfast in India and one they would remember. This morning there were stuffed parathas. They followed these with small portions of zarga – sweet rice with fruits and nuts. Finally coffees came. This morning they both had cappuccinos.

There was just time to pack everything and go to the airport.

"Don't forget the blue bag. It has our wedding clothes in it."

"Ok here it is," Cary said as he heaved it out of the wardrobe. The other case was put on the bed and gradually filled. Cary made a final tour of the bathroom and bedroom. They seemed to have everything. Leaving the bags in the room they went down to check out. A trolley with their baggage appeared. Cary settled up and they stepped outside just as a taxi was drawing up.

"Airport please", Cary said as they loaded. Soon, they had said good-bye and were speeding towards the highway.

Suddenly the taxi driver jammed on his brakes. Both Cary and Vee jerked forwards but saved themselves from being hurt. They noticed there was a cow in the road and it didn't seem to be in a hurry. The cow turned one way, then the other, before starting a slow walk. They started up again and all the traffic was suddenly back to normal. They then joined the main stream of traffic, on the

Highway. To the right, they noticed all the traffic had stopped for another cow, but their lane continued to move. Suddenly, a car approaching them decided to turn right so just turned, in front of them. Their driver was quick to notice and managed to brake in time. They then continued. They were nearly at the airport, but there was an elephant in front of them. They had to slow right down. It was just possible to squeeze past this ambling creature and then speed on. The driver took them straight to Departures. They got out and took a trolley. He then loaded their bags onto the trolley. Cary paid him and they wished him good luck. All they had to do, was find the Thai Airways flight to Bangkok. They joined the queue and eventually checked in. They waited in the seating area, for the flight to be called and gate opened. Suddenly, there was an announcement in a strange language and a rush. They left the building and boarded the plane.

Sitting on the plane, chat started.

"Well Christmas is coming soon, I feel like going to a church."

"Well, I was brought up as a Buddhist."

"I know, but you could try it, couldn't you?"

"Yes, my love, of course I could. Which church do you want to go to?"

"Good question. I thought we might check out that place where we got married. We'll just pop in to see what times the Christmas services are."

"Ok."

The food came round. It was not very appetizing. They both poked and prodded it and ate small samples here and there, like a bird. Then coffee came. It was not particularly fresh.

"Anyway we'll be landing soon." Sure enough, no sooner had Cary spoken than there was an announcement about safety belts and landing information. As soon as the plane touched down, they were relieved to be back in Thailand – the land where they were always so busy, but it was home!

From the Airport they took a taxi to 'Cary and Vees' in Pattaya.

The taxi pulled up. Cary paid and they entered the restaurant. SooSoo and Jira spotted them and went straight to them, to report that everything was running smoothly. Even though Tan's older sister, Noon, had temporarily left the staff, takings seemed to increase daily. Another new-comer, Pla, was doing very well. She now had found herself her own flat. SooSoo remained on the till and Jira kept his eye on everything else. The whole place was ticking over without them physically taking part. Cary and Vee left their bank details with Jira, so that they could receive income on paydays. But they were delighted to be able to leave the place to run itself – that is, in the capable hands of SooSoo and Jira. Cary and Vee left.

They then went to see the priest at their church.

"Oh hello, I remember you two!"

"Cary and Vee – we have just come to check the timings of your Christmas Services."

ORGANIC

"Well, I am sorry but I don't know what, if any, services we will have. Our poor organist has come down with a terrible virus of some sort. They have him in the hospital. So that's it. No music.

"I can play your organ for you if you like. I was a trombonist with GSO (Guildford Symphony Orchestra) but I did an Organ Scholarship when I was a student."

"Oh that's splendid! When can you start?"

"Well, could I have a little practice?"

"Of course, you're welcome, just go ahead. That's the switch over there."

Vee took a seat in the pew and Cary climbed up to the console. He started to play from memory some of Bach's Choral Preludes.

Vee listened with rapt attention. It was unlike anything she had ever heard before in her life and she absorbed and wallowed in its sombre beauty.

After 3 or 4 pieces Cary climbed down and switched off. The priest handed him a list of proposed Services and timings.

"Will you be able to help with all of these?"

Cary checked it carefully.

"Yes, I think so." Cary and the Priest shook hands. Vee was delighted to have discovered yet another of the pleasures that Cary was capable of giving her.

YUMMY AGAIN!

"Hey we haven't had any lunch yet! Aren't you hungry?"

"Well, now you mention it, yes I am.

They took a taxi to ''Indian by Nature''.

It was an opportunity to enjoy, again, the best Indian food available in Pattaya

Cary and Vee ordered Tarka Dahl, Rogan Josh and two vegetable biryanis. They were both too full for any desserts. They asked for two cappuccinos.

When outside, they walked towards the seafront.

"The air always seems fresher at the seafront."

"That's because of the negative ions."

"You know about everything don't you?"

"I don't know much about negative ions or the history of Peloponnesia ."

"What about the history of Thailand?"

"Oh I'm a great authority on that."

"Really?"

"Oh yes – breathe this fresh air."

"All right. It's very nice."

"You get negative ions when a lot of water and a lot of air mix."

"Ok"

"Taxi time?"

"Ya."

They were soon back at their apartment after quite an exhausting day.

Cary knew he would be wanted at the Church, in 2 days' time.

CARY AND VEE with confidence

With the usual preparations completed they again found themselves side by side in bed, body to body. Holding hands, they slept.

It was after mid-day when they awoke. They were both overcome by the need to rest, spending a lazy afternoon at their condotel.

Suddenly, it was 'get-up and go' time.

Cary put a CD on. They were in the mood for coming together. Preparations were made and clothes were removed. All the time Cary and Vee remained eyes to eyes.

"This is what I do and this is how I do it," they were saying to each other silently as they disrobed, unbuttoned, took off, pulled down with concentration and inspiration from eyes, as if they were saying

"Do this!" or "Do that!" The music seemed to go with it and Vee wondered what it might be called,

"Bolero" she was told, "By Maurice Ravel." Vee's reply was to throw herself on to the bed. Cary scrambled after her pretending to be a wild animal. They met in an energized embrace which stopped and started in time with the music.

They came together in intimacy. Vee's eyes closed with pleasure as Cary began his preparations for the finale. Vee's eyes opened and as she jolted - she screamed and wriggled. Cary was just in time for the Finale of heaving and gasping. They managed to reach a 3-part climax and both were highly amused by their success.

After some relaxation, they prepared for a walk along the sea-front. Then Cary's phone rang. He was needed at 8.30am tomorrow to play the organ, for the 9am service. He accepted immediately and told Vee.

"On the way home I will have to go with my passport to the Police Station, but won't take long."

Hand in hand they enjoyed the setting sun together. This walk seemed so relaxing and pleasant to them both. Only after some time, did they have the inclination, to turn back to their hotel.

It was an early night for both. Vee knew that Cary had to be out early.

DOOMED MORNING

At the appointed hour Cary rose and got himself ready.

"Bye-bye my love, good luck," she murmured from her bed. He leant over her, to kiss good-bye, then left.

Vee was overcome by a sense of uneasiness, being totally alone in the room. Surely, she should have gone with him. For some reason she felt guilty of not showing him support when it was her duty to give it. She got herself ready and went down to a lonely breakfast. She could do no more than peck at the fresh papaya.

"Mr. Cary okay Miss?" the waiter asked.

"Yes thanks. Very busy this morning." She had the terrible feeling that she was lying to him but her brain said, 'don't be silly - that was a very fair question to ask and your answer was quite reasonable.' She ordered a cappuccino. It was just after 8.30 now, she noticed. Cary would be at the Church and getting ready to play. Vee made her way back upstairs and prepared herself for going out. Why? - She didn't know, but she could not stay longer, alone, in that room! Suddenly another realization came to her. Her period had been due two days ago, but it hadn't come – 'I must be pregnant!' she told herself, with a mixture of joy and alarm. It was now nearly 10.30am. Cary had said he would be home at 10 o'clock. It was not like him to be late.

'What could be the problem? Why am I worried about this? she puzzled. Suddenly her phone rang. It was her mother.

"Vee my love," she began in Thai, "I am deeply sorry. Dear Cary has left this world." At this news Vee collapsed in tears. "Are you sure you know what you are talking about?" she asked angrily.

"I never wanted to give you this news, but I had to tell you. He was in a traffic accident – that is all I can say."

Vee was still sobbing when there was a knocking at her door. It was her mother. She entered and a Thai Police

Officer waited outside. There was some intensive talking between the two women. Eventually, Madame Dee said,

"They want you to identify the body." Vee composed herself and got ready. They left the Hotel accompanied by the Thai Officer. Both women got into the Police car and it sped off. They came to a downtown building with a flat roof. It was next to the Police Department. The car pulled up and they went in, following the Police Officer. They entered a very cold room in which there were stretchers all over the floor. On each one, was some sort of injured but motionless corpse. The Police Officer went straight to one of them. Vee looked and saw that the blood-stained contorted figure before her was HER CARY, Again she collapsed in tears, but struggled to control herself.

"Yes," said Madame Dee, sombrely, in Thai, to the Police Officer, "This is Mr. Cary Simmonds."

"You will receive a letter from his lawyer in a few days." The two women muttered their thanks and left the building.

"Let me take you back to your Hotel," the Police Officer called to them. Minutes later they were swooping towards their Condotel.

Vee's smile to him was almost painful. Her world had fallen apart.

Her mother could not console her, much as she tried. Madame Dee went off to get some shopping.

Vee struggled to compose herself, alone in the comfort of the Condotel. She asked herself what Cary's advice would be in a situation like this – as if he were here (and, of course not here) at the same time. The result of this exercise was to boost her spirits and make her feel that optimism was justified. She was confused, to say the least. She sat, calmly enjoying these thoughts, when it suddenly came to her that Cary's answer in all moments of need, was to pray – and she learned in the Church that (the Christian) God loves us and wants to bring happiness to our lives. 'Well, my mum thinks I am Buddhist and that's what I've always been,' she mused.

Then she was gripped by the urge to act – she had decided to Pray to God and ask for help. Vee closed her eyes and began her desperate request. Tears came and fell slowly, as she described her situation.

"Please help me," she intoned in simple English. The little thing inside her was just beginning to grow.

'Why should my baby suffer?' she wondered as so many of her sisters before her had done.

VEE'S COURAGE

So it was Vee, with a spring in her step. Absolutely no answers to her problems, but a germ of faith within her, growing faster than the little one. She walked towards the beach where, long ago, she met Rob. He and Cary had been different men, but she had loved then both.

There was a new café on the beach now. She stopped for a coffee. A farang man about Cary's age sat opposite.

"Excuse me, do you speak English?"

"Yes, I do."

"Live around here?"

"Quite near."

"By the way, my name's Jack," he said, offering his hand, "Jack Costain"

"My name's Viraporn Willapana, but you can call me Vee,"

"My first time in Thailand," Jack added, not wanting to ask about work.

"Would you like me to be your Tour Guide, I'm not expensive?"

"Ok, thank you. That would be very helpful. Is there anything *I* could do to help *you*?"

"Well, it doesn't matter if you can't help. My husband has just died in a road accident and I am pregnant. I was devastated so I just did what he would have done and prayed."

"So you are not a Buddhist?"

"Well, I'm getting a taste for Christianity."

"That's good! – I mean, I work for a Radio Station called Hope Radio. All the Broadcasts are Christian. It is operated by an organization called the YMCA, which is a Christian Charity in the UK."

"So you are Christian?"

"That's right!"

Suddenly Vee's mobile rang. It was the Priest from the Church where she and Cary were married. She had to tell him the news to explain why he did not turn up, to play the organ, as arranged. Vee apologized to him.

"How long are you in Thailand, Jack?"

"May be a few weeks, maybe more. I'm just getting a feel for it."

"Will you be here tomorrow? I enjoyed talking to you and it would be nice to meet you again."

"Oh yes. I come here most days."

Vee left Jack and continued her walk. 'What's this?' she asked herself, 'Not *another* café table with *another* farang!'

This one was chubbier than Jack and had very short hair with a beard and moustache. Vee wasn't keen on the idea of another coffee so she ordered a juice.

"Hi!" they both said together.

"Where are you from?" Vee began.

"Besancon, France, but I have lived all my life in England in a place called, Chichester."

"Are you bi-lingual then? – I mean English and French?"

"No, I don't remember much French and I am now trying to learn Thai."

"May be I could teach you."

"Ok, but you know what I really miss in Thailand?"

"No."

"Playing the organ." I used to play, every day, in Chichester Cathedral."

Vees brain was racing.

"Could you play the organ for services in a Church?"

"Oh yes – of course I could – that's easy!"

Vee phoned the priest and handed her phone to him.

"Tell him you want to play his organ."

An animated conversation followed. He took notes of times and address.

"Wow, thanks for that! – Danni Harper," he said, offering his hand.

Vee responded, introducing herself.

"Well I ought to do something for *you* – please let me know if there is anything."

Vee then told this farang of her predicament. He seemed always to have laughing eyes. She wondered if he was trustworthy. Vee suddenly decided to put it to the test. Leaving her purse on the table (it contained only about 1000 to 1500 Baht and some old receipts) she excused herself and went off to the ladies' room. She returned, ready for anything.

Danni sat waiting for her and the purse lay where she had left it, unmoved.

"By the way Danni. I told you I prayed."

"Yes?"

"Well, does that mean anything to you?"

"Yes of course. I often pray myself. I am Christian, you know – but I suppose you are Buddhist?"

Vee gave her standard reply.

Will you be in the Church when I am playing the organ?

Vee looked at him.

"Yes"

"Will you be with me when I am having my baby?"

"Yes, I will. I wouldn't miss it for anything."

VEE AND DANNI

Vee's phone rang. This time it was Cary's Lawyer. Money left by him had been transferred to her account.

"Let's go for lunch somewhere. They took a taxi. Vee stopped at the bank to pick up her new credit card and get the PIN. Vee then took Danni to 'Cary and Vees'.

"See how you like this."

They were all pleased to see her. There were hugs, kisses and commiserations from all and sundry. Vee introduced Danni and then sat with him to order.

"This is the restaurant I started with my late husband."

"So that's what you do for a living – a restauranteur?"

"Yes that's it, but I do it solo now, which is quite nice – I get 2 salaries!"

"May be you could use some help? - I used to work in a coffee bar, if that's any good."

"I am sure they would welcome you, they already seem to like you."

"That's good, but I would only need to look in now and then, yes?"

"Quite right, they run the place themselves. It's our job just to keep an eye on it so that it goes on paying us." Danni smiled at his new-found professional career.

Vee then introduced Danni as the new partner.

"Replacing Mr. Cary," she explained.

"Vee, I am a bit concerned, because your late husband Cary died recently."

"Yes, that's correct, why are you mentioning it now?"

"Well, what about his funeral?"

"Oh my God! Yes! Thank you dear Danni for reminding me. Vee called again to her Lawyer to ask him about it. He said the date and time had been set and it would be at the same cemetery as was, his brother, Rob's Funeral. 4.00pm on Tuesday 18th November. Vee checked her Funeral clothes and Danni said he would buy some.

"I suppose I'll have to write a speech," Danni added,

unenthusiastically.

As they left the restaurant Vee asked Danni where he was living. He said that it was in an apartment off Soi Burkao, as he was living at the moment, for economy. Danni confided that he had a wealthy uncle who was currently in hospital with a bout of flu. This man and Danni had been very close all their lives. He was expecting a generous inheritance from him.

"When did you last see him?"

"About 2 weeks ago, just before coming to Thailand. I'll go back again soon."

"Would you care to have lunch with me?"

"Well I am a bit short myself."

"Yes, I realise that – but *I* 'm inviting *you.*"

"That's very kind of you. Where shall we go?"

"I think I have a place in mind. By the way, I'm vegetarian."

"Brilliant! So am I!"

"Well let's go to my favourite Indian Restaurant in Pattaya."

"Perfect. But, are you forgetting, I have to play the organ at the morning service first?"

"Oh dear, I quite forgot, yes and you had better not be late."

They took a taxi to the Church.

DANNI - Organist

Danni was in time. People were still arriving at the church. He quickly switched on and mounted the organ seat. He began to play quietly as Vee and others, found themselves seats. The service proceeded in the normal way for Danni. For Vee it was a new experience. It was a mixture of songs, which everyone else seemed to know. There were prayers in a strange form of English. Vee knew that her English was 'not good enough for prayers.' During the service, people started queuing so that they could go up to the altar. Vee wondered what that was about, but when she was asked she stood up and joined the queue. Like the other people she knelt at the altar. The priest came to her and touching her head said, "God Bless you." The other people were getting a wafer and a sip of wine, but Vee knew from the prayers what this represented. She knew she had to get some information about it. Like the others she stood and returned to her place. Danni was playing again. It went on for about an hour. When Danni finally finished, he came to Vee.

"Again tomorrow afternoon," he announced, "then next week Friday and Sunday." Vee was not as enthralled as usual but she was happy to be Danni's supporter, so she smiled and said,

"Good!"

They took a taxi to, "'Indian by Nature'," the restaurant that Vee recommended.

For Vee it was strange being in the driving seat with money, but she didn't mind paying for this man. Something about him, impressed her. In some ways he was very much like Cary – physically, of course, quite different.

As they entered Danni was entranced.

"This décor and the music make me feel I am back in India."

"Oh, you have been to India?"

"Yes, but quite a long time ago."

At the restaurant they both took pleasure in examining the gigantic menu. They sat at the grand table like a Maharajah and his Maharani selecting exotic purchases from a special catalogue.

Eventually the waiter came. Questions were answered and orders taken.

"Do you want a beer or wine?" Vee asked tentatively.

"Not for me, thanks." Vee was relieved.

During the meal Vee decided to tell Danni the story of how she met Jack and the arrangement she had made to meet him again, tomorrow.

"I want you to know that I value your friendship more than his and after our meeting tomorrow I have no wish to see him again. It is you Danni, I want to see again."

"Well, I tell myself I am broad-minded and now I have a chance to prove it. Actually, I am glad because I certainly would like to see you again."

They finished with some Indian sweets. They both chose Gulab Jamon. Then there were coffees.

"Let me show you where I live." They took a taxi to Vee's Condotel apartment. She explained to Danni about the Condotel arrangement.

"Well this is my place," Vee gave him the Hotel Card and said,

"Just call and ask for extension 72"

"Good luck with Jack. I hope to see you tomorrow."

"Thank you. Me too."

Vee was feeling much better. The prayers she said, had certainly produced results – more than she had expected. She went down to the foyer and found that another episode of The Oshin Story was just starting. She sat and watched. Oshin was learning to do ladies' hair. She was the kind of girl who picked it up fast and many wealthy customers tipped her. Another lady noticed Oshin. She was the boss of the shop, who had taught her. Realising how quickly she had learned, she decided to take Oshin under her wing, as a personal friend. Vee's phone rang. It was Danni, just

163

to say, he would soon be going to the airport to fly to the UK.

Vee returned to her room, but for the first time, she did not mind solitude. It gave her a certain freedom. She prayed to thank God for answering her prayers so abruptly and generously.

She also prayed for the souls of Rob and Cary. She realised, perhaps for the first time, what a huge part those men had played in her life and education. Cary had given her the ultimate gift – her baby.

On a whim she called International Directories and asked for Hope Radio. She wrote the number on an envelope on the desk, then called.

"Good morning, I have a message for someone who works for you."

"His name?, yes, it's Jack Costain,"

"Jack who? Wait a minute – I know that name. He joined us about 3 years ago but he left after only a few days with us – are you sure you want Jack Costain?"

"No, I am not sure. Thank you for your information. Good-bye." Vee was not perturbed by this news. Thoughts about Danni soon returned to her mind.

It was a sweet-smelling, clean and relaxed Vee who returned from the bathroom to her bed. She was only very slightly bigger.

VEE BUSINESS

As morning came, Vee prepared herself and went down to breakfast. She thought she had better tell the Hotel that this Condo had passed into her name, so she started, by going to the desk and giving them her bank details.

She called Carry's Lawyer to tell him she wanted to sell the Condo and ask him to handle it for her. She also called all the employees of Cary & Vee's to tell them about the funeral and wake. It would be one day, off-work, for the restaurant.

During breakfast, she began to think about her planned liaison this morning.

Vee knew, she had no excuse not to go and meet him.

When she had prepared herself for going out, she walked down toward the beach. Jack had been at the first table. She saw it ahead of her. There was nobody there. She approached and sat down.

The waiter came.

"Excuse me Mam, your name is Vee?"

"Yes, how did you know?"

"I was asked by a farang to give you this note."

"Dear Vee, It was great to meet you. Sorry I cannot be with you today. Duty calls – I have to rush back to England to my job at Hope Radio. The waiter here will tell you when I am back in Thailand again. Take Care – Jack."

'So Jack is a man who cannot speak the truth – Cannot be a Christian!' Vee found herself thinking.

She returned to the main road and took a taxi to Soi Burkao. She thought she would try to find Danni.

Having had enough rushing about for one morning she entered a bar and asked for an iced tea. A figure appeared at the doorway.

"Hi, Is that you, Vee?"

"Oh, Danni, you are here!"

"Yes this is the area where I live." Danni ordered an orange juice.

"You must come and see what a terrible place I have."

Vee had to laugh.

"I'm sure it's not terrible."

She followed Danni from the bar and soon they were walking up the Soi. There was a forecourt with cars and bikes. She followed Danni up the stairs. He opened his door.

"Welcome to my home sweet home,"

Vee beheld the untidy mess before her. This was not a Hotel room regularly cleaned, swept and polished, by an industrious staff. This was just a room with basics – bed – fridge – cooking ring. Radio/CD player and wardrobe.

"In there is the bathroom," Danni said, pointing.

"Church this afternoon – coming with me?"

"Of course, what time?"

"We leave at 5o'clock."

"Ok, I'll be ready."

"Then we do Friday and Sunday. I was going back to England on Monday. I'll change it to Wednesday, because of Cary's Funeral. My visa is running out and I have to visit my uncle and others in my family."

"So, when you come back phone me and I'll meet you at the airport. Ok, this is my number, don't forget, please."

"No, I won't. I promise I will phone you, Vee, it will be in about 2 or 3   weeks, but I *will* phone you."

"Want to have lunch with me?"

"Ok, but next time, I'll pay."

They walked up to Third Road and got a taxi to 'Cary & Vees'.

"We'll have to change the name now" Vee announced as they arrived.

"You mean just, 'Vee's Café?'"

"I suppose so, but why not just leave it for now? Many people knew Cary"

"I think you are right."

VEE AND DANNI - at work

Tarrin came to tell them he had attracted the interest of a movie company. Apparently they wanted someone like him to do Muay Thai (Thai Boxing).

"If I am not here, I think Orn can take over and will soon learn the job."

"Well congratulations and I'll have a word with Orn anyway."

"Hey, Orn, can you spare a minute?"

"Hello Mr Danni, Sir, how can I help you?" Orn was a woman of more muscular figure than Vee and a plain-looking face. She wore jeans, a loose top and plain shoes. Danni was impressed with her politeness and decided she should be given a chance.

"Orn, can you take over Tarrin's job when he is away – he has an important assignment?"

"Yes Sir. No problem. I will do that, for sure."

"Thank you Orn and welcome to 'Cary & Vee's' Restaurant."

"Thank you Sir!"

They placed their orders for food. There were many vegetarian options, Vegetable Green Curry, Pad Thai Vegetables or Pak Ruam Mit… They ordered one Pad Thai and a Green Curry. Vee suddenly noticed the woman who had entered the restaurant. Vee's face clouded over. She realised this was the woman who had refused to pay because the food had too much chilli for her. Vee decided to give her some education. She invited her to come to the kitchen.

"Seriously, if you are allergic to chilli, you should not ever eat Thai food. There is no escape from the taste of chilli. It is on the knife and spoon that have touched the chilli. It is on the plate or bowl that has had chillies on it. If you are sensitive to chillies, you will always notice them."

"Oh Madame, thank you for understanding me. I am so sorry I complained about your restaurant. People think I am crazy, because they love it here."

"Thank you, but you are not crazy. There are many types of food allergy and they are perfectly serious to those who have them – Peanuts and strawberries, for example - If you would care to stay here, how about a Thai dessert and a cup of tea?" The woman smiled and agreed to stay.

"Lot-tong, la ko, cha ron," Vee said to the waiter as the woman sat down.

"When are you due, dear?" she enquired.

"Oh, about 7 or 8 months," Vee replied, almost having forgotten. She returned to her table with Danni.

"That was a smooth move."

"Thank you, she was a real pain the first time she came, so I wanted to make her feel more at home here."

"And you succeeded!"

"Don't forget – tomorrow CLOSE – it's Mr Cary's funeral tomorrow and everyone must come."

"Yes, we know," Jira replied

They then left and went home to the Condo

Unbeknown to Vee, Danni was using his time not only for packing, but also to write the Funeral Speech.

THE FUNERAL OF CARY SIMMONDS

"Dear Friends, It is an honour and privilege for me to be able to say a few words about a formidably kind, sensitive and artistic man, with whom I had no physical acquaintance. I have to tell you how impressed I am, since I have been given a familiarity with Cary, by the woman God has given to me, to love and hold. She has conveyed to me the profound love and respect she had for this man, who devoted himself to her. I personally feel strong empathy with him. It is a tragic act of destiny, that has deprived Cary of knowing his child.

I hereby, swear to all you who hear me, that I will be the best father I can to this little one, whether male or female, even though I am not his or her biological father, as God is my Witness!

It remains for me to apologise for practically ignoring you good people who have come here today. I must thank you for wishing to show your respect to him by your memory of him – Cary Simmonds - a Great Musician and a Great Man!"

When he had finished Vee was asleep.

Next morning they followed the same routine as for Rob's Funeral and got themselves suitably dressed. Vee had a black skirt and white blouse. Danni had a black suit, white shirt and black tie. They both looked very smart, in a serious sort of way. They had a small breakfast on the ground floor. This was a day to be given to Cary. They were both totally committed to this cause.

"O my love, what about the speech?"

"Don't worry. I did it last night when you were asleep."

"Good. You are not the kind of man to forget something like that."

"Thank you, darling."

They got a taxi to Charoen Krung Road Protestant

Cemetery. Many other taxis and cars arrived at the same location. They waited and a large black car approached slowly. When it parked, the coffin was rolled out and Danni joined those who were the bearers. It was carried into the cemetery by a group of sombre-faced men. Danni got his speech ready.

"Dear Friends, It is an honour and privilege for me to be able to say a few words about a formidably kind, sensitive and artistic man, with whom I had no physical acquaintance. I have to tell you how impressed I am, since I have been given a familiarity with Cary, by the woman God has given to me, to love and to hold. She has conveyed to me, the profound love and respect she had for this man, who devoted himself to her. I personally feel strong empathy with him. It is a tragic act of destiny, that has deprived Cary of knowing his child.

I hereby, swear to all you who hear me, that I will be the best father I can to this little one, whether male or female, even though I am not his or her biological father, as God is my Witness! If any man deserves this service – Cary does

It remains for me to apologise for practically ignoring all you good people who have come here today. I must thank you, for wishing to show your respect to him by your kind gestures and memory of him – Mr Cary Simmonds – a Great Musician and a Great Man!"

This speech was greeted with strong, earnest applause. The priest then took over and prayers were said. Finally, the moment arrived when both Vee and then Danni threw earth on to the, now lowered, coffin. The words,

"Earth to Earth and Dust to Dust," were solemnly intoned. Vee had now performed her last act for Cary. She was sad and tearful as she and Danni turned away. Danni held her quietly, and felt the deep sorrow that was affecting her. When he felt she had recovered slightly, he began,

"I didn't ask you, my love. What did you think of my speech? Was it all right? - It's very difficult to write a speech about someone you have never met."

"Yes, my love. It was perfect. You did a very good job, as you always do."

There was an announcement about 'the wake at the Landmark Hotel.' Cars and taxis were put to use.

There was a well-designed spread of all kinds of appealing food. The Landmark had set it all up at very short notice. Danni provided some music with his CD player. He said,

"This is the way Cary would like to celebrate and knowing Cary, it is his aim to see everyone happy and having a good time!" Soo and Jira were there. Prem and Borant showed their respects. Far and Tan were there, also Tarrin and Orn. Lek appeared with Noon. Everyone looked sombre in their funeral garbs, but then Danni played some lively music and couples started dancing. There was also some wine available. Celebrations were thus lubricated and it went on and on. It was quite late when people finally started to leave

Vee and Danni then said their farewells.

"10 am tomorrow and 8 pm Sunday," Danni suddenly said.

DANNI, VEE and CHRISTIANITY

Vee was aware of being bigger that before. She decided to invite Danni to her Condotel. Danni said he would need to move all his luggage from Soi Burkao. He took a taxi then filled it with his stuff. He checked out at the office and drove off with the taxi. Soon all his things were installed in the Condotel. They both rested. Morning came, and the 'busyness' started. They went down to breakfast. By 9.30 they had finished and prepared to leave. Vee was determined to accompany Danni and not repeat the mistake she made with poor Cary. They took a limousine and arrived at the Church at just on 10. Danni had time to start playing before people arrived and Vee knew the routine. This time it was songs and prayers, then the queueing and more prayers and songs. Finally, the Priest blessed everybody. Vee waited for Danni to be ready.

Back at the hotel, Vee asked Danni about the queuing and the wafers and wine.

"The wafers represent Christ's body and the wine represents His blood."

In the Bible, we are told that at the Last Supper – Jesus said,

"This is my body - take and eat this bread in remembrance – of me" Then He said, (holding the wine)

"This is my blood, which is shed for you and for many, to enable forgiveness of your sins." Christian people believe they are doing their duty to God, by sharing in this symbolic last supper with Jesus Christ. It brings them spiritual strength and sometimes, healing"

"Can I do this?"

"Yes. Of course, if you believe it. It's called 'Holy Communion' or 'The Eucharist.'"

"You sound like a priest."

"That's because ordinary people don't talk about these things."

They returned to their hotel and got changed for a swim.

They went to the Hotel pool. It was an invitation to a splashing contest and then serious swimming started. Vee now looked bigger but she could certainly swim well. Danni was attentive to her in-case she got into difficulties. But all seemed to go well. It was exercise that they both needed. A huge coloured ball splatted down in front of Vee and she threw it back to the children it came from. It was time to get out and dry. Wrapped in towels they returned to their condo and freshened up for an evening meal.

"This time tomorrow will be the last time before I go."

"What do you mean, go where?"

"I told you I have to go back to England on Monday to visit my uncle and others in the family."

"Oh, yes, sorry, I forgot."

"You won't forget to phone me when you come back, will you?

"No, I never forget anything!"

"Clever you! Pass me the salt please."

They were enjoying fish and chips.

"This is not exactly vegetarian, but ok just once, I think"

"Me too."

Vee and Danni rested. They were content and at ease, in each other's company. As tiredness overcame them they went to bed.

Next morning, they started as usual. It was their last day together.

Danni decided to show Vee his Bible. His was NKJ – (New King James) this was a more modern type of English than the King James (KJ) version. He explained that most of the Church Service was taken from the KJ version so it was difficult to understand. He showed Vee the part about the Last Supper and then he gave it to her. She could see that it had a useful index at the back.

So they were late at breakfast, but there were still dishes to choose from and they finished with cappuccinos.

Most of the morning passed with Vee reading assiduously, her newly acquired Bible. Danni didn't want to interrupt her so he bought a newspaper and checked the Sudoku puzzle.

"Let's go down to the beach," Danni suddenly said.

"Ok." Vee went to change and Danni did the same. They walked down to the Sea front and began walking along the beach.

They reached a table and there was already someone there.

"Jack!" Vee said in surprise.

"Oh, hello – fancy seeing you"

"This is Danni"

"Jack, how are you?"

"Hello Danni."

"Good thanks." The waiter came and Danni bought drinks for Vee and himself. Jack ordered a Pepsi.

"Did you really go to England Jack?"

"Well I told you in my letter, didn't I?"

"Yes, but you lied to me."

"What do you mean?"

"You didn't work for Hope Radio – you started there a few years ago, then left."

"What are you Police or Inland Revenue?"

"Neither – I am someone who expects to be told the truth – and I am, usually."

"Does she argue with everyone like this?"

"I think you better be careful what you are saying," Danni warned him.

"Oh, another thing, Jack. Do you want to be a Christian?"

Jack laughed. Danni and Vee left the table and found the waiter to pay him. They then walked away, back to Vee's Condo.

It was late lunch time. They selected from the buffet. And went to sit. Danni began to offer a prayer of thanks. Vee noticed and did the same. It was very enjoyable and they finished with coffees. In the Condo, Danni made sure that Vee took her Bible and returned to his newspaper for a while. They were due to leave at 7pm. Danni already had his ticket and most of his packing done for tomorrow.

They arrived at the church in good time. Both Danni and Vee knew their routines. It was just songs and prayers today. They both agreed to pray for Jack. It all went smoothly. The Priest again blessed everyone. As they were leaving he rushed up to them.

"Thank you so much for helping us. I don't know how you do it, my dear Vee, but you found us another organist so quickly, it was a miracle."

"Well, just let me know if there is anything else I can do for you."

They made their way back to the Condotel.

DANNI GOES TO THE UK

"Airport tomorrow," Danni suddenly said.

"Oh, yes, so it is! What time's your flight? I'll come and see you off."

"11am, so it's check in at 9 am."

"I don't think I can get up that early."

Danni and Vee stared at each other. Then Vee began to laugh.

"I was just joking. We'll go to the airport together - I'll be ready at about 7.45" Then they went to their Condo.

Next morning Vee had an alarm call. She got herself ready. Danni woke up and was soon ready. They had an early breakfast. Back in the condo, Danni appeared with his flight bag and quite a large suitcase. Vee phoned for a taxi to pick them up. Someone came to take Danni's luggage down. Danni tipped them.

"It's ok, I am coming back," Vee said to the receptionist. Moments later a car swooped up to them and stopped.

"Airport, please – Suvarnebhumi," The fare of 600 was agreed and they were soon on the Tollway heading West.

"How long do you think you will be in England?"

"Well, I would like to say, 2 weeks, but it could be as much as 4 weeks. I am sure my Uncle will be delighted to see me. I would like him to be happy and enjoy what he has left of life. He's disabled, so all the family share in taking care of him."

"What sort of disability?"

"He's blind. What he really loves is when I take him on walks. I try to find interesting places for him. When I'm not around he gets rather housebound and crotchety. He has only to hear my voice, to get himself into a better mood and come to life."

"So you are going to be busy. But I hope, not too busy to give me a call."

"Certainly I'll give you a call but it'll probably be in the afternoon for you, as I am not likely to be awake at 3 am."

"Can I call you?"

"Sure, of course you can. The UK is currently 6 hours earlier than Thailand."

"Departures?" the driver asked.

"Yes, please."

Talking stopped. They both realised that this was the Airport. The taxi came to a halt. Danni paid and the driver helped unload. Danni went to get a trolley then loaded it. He and Vee pushed together. He found the Eva Air desk and joined the queue. He turned to Vee.

"Ok, sweetie, Thanks for coming with me. We'll keep in touch and I very much hope to see you soon."

"Me too," Vee replied with a sunshine smile. She turned to go. Vee marched towards the exit but she turned round for one last look at him. She found him staring straight at her – Danni had watched her walk away – They both waved enthusiastically and exchanged smiles. Then he had to go, so she went too.

Vee started to wonder how she would handle this quiet time ahead. 'I suppose if I was middle-aged, I would take up knitting.' She decided to go to the restaurant and pitch in with what ever was needed. She found them as busy as ever. Jira was alone at the cash till. He said that SooSoo had fever so she had to stay home. Vee looked in the kitchen to see how it was going. She then checked upstairs. Only a few of the tables up there were taken. Tarrin asked her to go out and buy coconuts – about 8 or 10. Vee took a large string bag. It was satisfying for her to have something useful to do with herself. She returned with the coconuts, the bill and change. She then sat herself down to lunch. Fresh Green Curry with vegetables and rice.

She then had mango and sticky rice, followed by a coffee.

On the way out she asked Jira,

"Wouldn't it be cheaper to use those packets of coconut powder instead of all the preparation of fresh coconuts?"

"Yes, cheaper and quicker, but that packet stuff contains maltodextrin – many customers are not keen on that."

Vee was impressed with Jira's prompt informative reply.

VEE MOVES

As she sat in the Hotel, waiting for another episode of 'Oshin' to start, Vee suddenly thought how absurd it was to be paying for a whole Condo, just for herself. Oshin was just starting so she watched it all. She had a baby now. She had to take him with her where ever she was working. She had met a friendly man who had taken advantage of her. However, he considered he should give her something in return. He risked his life by conveying to her a highly secret custom of the Yakusa (Japan's Mafia). She never forgot this strange posture nor betrayed its secrecy. She continued to work, cleaning and sweeping – anything she could get.

The episode finished and Vee immediately left, going to the building off Soi Burkao where Danni had lived. She called at the office. Yes, they could offer her a room on the second floor. The rent was agreed and with her small bag, she moved in. Vee then returned to the Condotel to check out. They agreed to contact her solicitor as soon as they had accepted an offer. All her things were packed and then carried for her downstairs. She took a taxi and said 'Goodbye' to the staff. In just minutes, the taxi was outside the building where she had her flat. Several lads appeared and helped her carry her luggage up to her room. She tipped each of them. Cary's Radio CD player was the first item to be unpacked. She put it on the shelf and plugged it in. There was news in Thai. It was a bit like being home with her brothers and mother – except that she was alone. She prayed for Danni, that he would have a safe flight and soon return to Thailand. She also prayed for her mother and brothers, Jira and Tarrin. She wondered what they might be doing now. Suddenly, her phone rang. It was her mother, (in Thai, of course)

"Where are you? What is going on? I called at your Hotel and they said you weren't there any more."

"No I've moved to a flat just off Soi Burkao, that a

friend told me about."

"You're a silly girl, slumming it. Why not come and stay with me?"

There was a pause.

"Your own bedroom, bathroom and office – it's far too big for me – I have to pay someone to clean it." Vee was waiting to speak.

"Thank you mother. That would be nice – Can I come tomorrow morning?"

Her mother agreed instantly and was clearly thrilled.

Vee then prepared for her one Soi Burkao night. No sheets – only blankets. Good hard bed. Ok, not noisy. Vee was tired and soon closed her eyes and slept.

The glaring sun woke her. The bathroom was basic. She got ready, realizing with disappointment that there was no place nearby waiting to serve her breakfast. It was check-out time. She got packed up again then went to the office. Vee was ready. She would offer him a week's rent. So she explained she was leaving and made her offer. Business was done. 'My mum will be cheaper too,' Vee told herself.

A taxi responded to her. The lads appeared again to help move her things. Again, she tipped them. She then told the driver 'Bang Na.' They swooped off.

Arriving in Bang Na housing estate they soon started checking the numbers. Outside one house a woman was waving.

"Yes that's the house and that's my Mum!" The taxi driver responded. He then helped unload and some local lads also helped. Suddenly there were boxes and bags with all Vee's luggage and all was quiet. A clock began striking. It was 9.45.

"Are you hungry?" Vee's mother asked.

"Yes, I am. I didn't have any breakfast."

"I thought as much, lucky I got you away from there, you might have starved."

Vee decided not to argue with her mother who was being very generous.

It didn't take her long to fill the table with a variety of Thai breakfast goodies and there was fresh rice soup. Vee was soon feeling much better and well nourished. She began moving her personal luggage into her rooms. When she saw the office, then the bathroom, then the bedroom, she began to feel her old self again. She felt totally relaxed. 'I must have been crazy going to Soi Burkao,' was the thought that came to her, just as there was a knocking on her door.

VEE WITH MUM

"Come in!" she called. It was her mother.

"I want to talk to you."

"Well?"

"Vee – you've changed. Something's come over you – but it's a good change. In a way you are more self-assured, stronger."

"So, at least I have improved."

"No, I just mean you have something that gives you brightness and vitality and I don't know what it is. I know it's not Gin Seng or anything like that.

I can tell you what it's not – but I can't tell you what it is. – Can you tell me?"

"Well, I am vegetarian and I am pregnant– I think those make some difference."

Madame Dee looked uneasy,

"No, dear, you have something and I want it. It's not a thing, I don't mean youth or money – something spiritual."

Vee thought about this. She knew what her mother meant but how could she explain?

"Well, as you know I have had a Farang partner and a Farang husband," she began.

"But there's another one now, isn't there?" Vee wondered how her mother could have known that.

"Yes, but I can never lose what those first two gave me. I was quite innocent and they influenced me. As a result I am Christian now.

"So your new man is Christian too?"

"Yes, he is."

Mother, you have been given a gift – like some people can heal, some can play a musical instrument, some excel at cooking etc but your gift, is an ability to see further than others – what you call, clairvoyance, I believe."

"Yes, that's right." Madame Dee realised her daughter was now, no innocent school dropout, but a sophisticated, well-educated young lady.

"There is a greater gift than this, available to anyone who asks for it."

"Oh, really, so who do I ask?
www.sendmemygift.com ?"

"No. This has been available for many years now, since before computers, phones and even before postal addresses. It's necessary to pray. I will pray with you if you like."

"Ok, thank you."

"There are two parts to this prayer. If you don't accept it or you don't like it. Just let me know and I'll cancel it. But let's try anyway. So, close your eyes, please, and think about what you are saying."

Vee then composed a prayer, which her mother repeated after her. The first part was to confess and ask forgiveness for all her errors, misdeeds, mistakes, jealousy, envy, misjudgement, moments of foolishness, anger, regret, worry etc. The second part was to affirm belief in and thanks for, the life of Jesus Christ which he gave, so that we could be saved." Madame Dee, closed her eyes and repeated Vee's words. She then embraced her daughter. This 'instant conversion' had, at least, a profound effect on this woman.

"Vee, my love, I don't know what I would do without you."

"You would run your business, helping people out of their troubles as a fortune teller."

"Yes, but may be, now, I can help them even more."

"You probably have the gift of healing too."

"Yes, I think that is quite possible, thank you."

"Remember to pray – you will ALWAYS get help – I do! Ok, so I am going to pray for lunch now."

"No need, I'm taking you out to lunch. I never thought I would have a daughter like you!"

Vee smiled. There was so much to be grateful for, here in this huge house, from the floral soap in the bathroom to the desk with laptop, fax and printer. Her phone rang. It was Danni.

184

"Hi Danni, how are you?"

"Vee, my love, I'm ok, but I am missing you. What's your news?"

"Me too, I mean, I am missing you too. I'm staying in Bang Na with my mum so I am feeling very posh here."

"Good, I know you are posh. I want to tell you about my Uncle Vic."

"Yes, ok darling, tell me."

"We went for a long walk yesterday and talked. Apparently he invented a new kind of Braille and patented it. He did it together with a friend. So they are now getting royalties from that. It's known as the 'Ross-Harper System.' It's doing well in Europe too, because it works with other languages. I knew he had some savings but he seems to have the Midas touch with finances. I let him be his own financial advisor. He is interested in things he can hear, like the sea, birds and music. I try to give him these sort of experiences."

"Seems you are being a good nephew to him."

"Yes, that's my duty at the moment. I hope I can see you soon. Something tells me I am in a 'win-win' situation."

"I think I see what you mean. It will be good to see you again, Take care."

"Me too. You take care. Bye!"

"Bye-bye, my love."

"Are you ready now?" Vee's mother called.

"Yes, just coming. My agent on the phone!"

Her mother gave her a look. The taxi was waiting. They both went to it and entered. Madame Dee told the driver, "'Indian by Nature'."

"Pattaya Madame?"

"That's right.

Not long afterwards mother and daughter faced each other across the table and contemplated the menu each had before them. They made their choices and the waiter took their order. Madame Dee was happy to be vegetarian with her daughter. They enjoyed the delightful food and both were able to take extra helpings from the bowls and dishes they particularly favoured. Vee had ordered chapattis. Her mother watched and copied as Vee scooped up vegetables with a piece of chapatti, then did the same again with rice and dahl. Spoons were also put to use. Vee ordered gulab jamon for dessert. She was sure her mother would enjoy it as much as her.

"Oh Gulab Jamon, yes I know this – I've had it before!" Madame Dee said as the waiter arrived with them.

"Please bring 2 portions of Rasgullah," Vee said.

"Yes Mam." The rasgullahs arrived.

"This too?"

"Yes, for you to try ok?"

"Yes, very good."

They both enjoyed their rasgullah.

They finished with coffees. Vee had cappuccino.

The two women continued to spend time together chatting endlessly on all the subjects that obsess the female mind. In this way several days were passed.

Then, one morning Vee's phone rang. It was Danni, again.

"Hello my love, how are you?"

"Still with my mum. She's saving me a lot of money, by putting me up."

"I have bad news."

"Oh I'm sorry. Your uncle I suppose – is he ok?"

"Well, he *was* ok, but he just didn't wake up this morning. The doctor came and pronounced him dead. He was nearly 90, so I suppose he had a good life."

"Was he born blind?"

"Oh no, it was an Army thing. A bomb blew up in his face. He got a special allowance from the MOD. He wrote in braille, about what it was like to suddenly go blind and how he adapted to it. The RNIB 'translated' it to plain English. It was quite a success with publishers and he got the Royalties from that too, of course. Tomorrow I will sort out his papers and see his solicitor. So I'll be back in

Thailand with you as soon as the funeral is over. I think that means next week, arrival in Bangkok."

"Ok I am really missing you Danni, but thank you for phoning me."

"Me too. I have to phone you because I can't go for long without hearing your voice."

"Well come back soon and you can hear me all the time."

"Yes, that's true. I will definitely do my best. Take care and God Bless you."

"Thank you and God Bless you too." Thai conversation:-

"Well that was an expensive call. Lover boy will have a huge phone bill."

"Don't worry. Some things are simply a good investment."

"I understand."

Vee's phone rang again. It was Cary's lawyer to say that her Condo had been sold for 100,000 more than Cary paid for it – so she would receive 700,000 Baht in her account.

THE NEW HEALER

So, the two women were living in each other's auras as only a mother and daughter can.

A woman from another house came to Madame Dee asking for help. She said she had breast cancer and the doctor said there were 3 tumors –

"Can you help me?" she asked. Madame Dee had never been in this situation before. She was surprised that this woman had come to *her* for help.

"I will try."

She took the woman into her room and placed her hands on the affected area of her breast. She closed her eyes and said a prayer asking the Holy Spirit 'to remove all Cancer and Tumours from this woman's body.'

"Ok. I believe you'll be alright now. Let me know how you are tomorrow and my fee is 500 Baht."

"Thank you," she replied handing over the money.

More days passed. It was time for more shopping. Madame Dee had phoned for a taxi. It came and they left the house. A man was waiting for them. He spoke English.

"Hello Thank you. My wife came to you the other day and now she is fine. The Doctor says she now has no tumors. You have an amazing gift! Thank you very much!"

"You are welcome Sir. My name is Madame Dee – I am a Healer. Just tell your friends."

"Thank you, I will." Thai conversation:-

"You people ready now?"

"Sorry to keep you waiting" They got in and the taxi zoomed off with a frustrated driver at the wheel.

"I must thank you Vee. You said I might be a healer and so I am!"

"I am happy for you mother. It is a valuable and unique gift."

Vee's phone rang. It was Jira.

"I seem to have picked up a bug from SooSoo and now

we are both unwell, how are you?" There were several coughs.

"I'm ok thank you. Why don't you two come to see my mother, she's a healer now?"

"What! - She can heal us, do you think?"

"If you believe she can."

"Sounds a bit like Voodoo."

"Actually it's the exact opposite. She heals you with the power of the Holy Spirit – Is that ok with you?"

"Sounds good to me."

"It is good – it's so good that there's nothing better."

"Can we come now – It's Bang Na where your mum lives, isn't it?"

"Just a minute." Vee told her mother about SooSoo and Jira.

"Tell them to come this evening, poor things," was her immediate response. Vee gave them the exact address. When they returned from shopping, she asked to watch TV as she wanted to see the next episode of 'Oshin.' They switched on and it had already started. Oshin was in a bar where some men were making trouble. She said to them,

"If you want to make trouble come outside with me."

A few men went outside and began laughing at her. She immediately adopted the Yakusa pose that she had been taught. When the men saw it they ran away in fear. So the now older, Oshin, was a woman known to have 'influence' on the street.

The doorbell rang. It was SooSoo and Jira. Madame Dee took them into her room. Vee continued watching TV. The programme finished. She switched it off and went to join the others.

Madame Dee's first observation of them was a well matched couple who seemed to suit each other like a hand and glove. Despite this, they both looked drawn, tired and rather exhausted. They were offered chairs. Vee sat quietly at the back. Madame Dee sat facing SooSoo and Jira. She asked them to close their eyes, but try not to go to sleep. She put a hand on to each of their heads and closed her

189

own eyes.

"In the name of the Holy Spirit, I banish all infirmity, inflammation, congestion and disease from these two children of God. Free them from all aches, all tiredness and restore them to perfect health." There was a pause.

"Ok –that's it. We've finished. We've done it!" They opened their eyes and managed smiles.

"My fee is 500 per person, so 1,000 for you 2." Jira reached into his pocket and opened his wallet, handing her a 1000 Baht note.

"Call me in 2 or 3 days" She told them as they left.

"I'm sure they will be ok by tomorrow," Vee said, as Madame Dee closed the door.

"The thing about healing, is that it makes me feel good. I feel I have done something useful."

"You have always been useful to me, mother."

"Yes, but I have no word, for what you are to me. I just wonder what other gift you will bring me next."

Vee and her mother embraced and kissed.

They stood looking in to eyes.

Then went to their rooms as night came.

Vee went to pray.

Madame Dee's phone rang. She sat on her bed. It was her client from Dubai, Masood. He wanted to come to see her again. This time he would bring his younger brother, Saleh. They made an appointment and she gave him her new address. She began to think about her responsibility for them. She decided that so long as she was honest with them, her usual services would be all right. Perhaps she would bring Masood good fortune again and give young Saleh a taste of her skills. She already had a good reputation in certain circles – but they didn't know she was Christian.

Madame Dee composed a plan in her mind for dealing with any question that might arise.

Vee's light was off. Now Madame Dee's went off.

Vee knew that it would be an exceptional morning. She

woke early and made a coffee with the machine in her room and cream from the fridge. She got herself ready and then emerged in search of breakfast. But her phone rang, so she returned to her room and closed the door. It was Danni. He simply couldn't stay away any longer so he was coming to Thailand. He had seen a copy of his Uncle's will and his solicitor would see that it was paid to his UK Bank account. He could access this online in Thailand.

So, Danni was due in Thailand this evening. She got his flight number and arrival time. She would go to meet him.

Vee left her room for a second time. Now, there was a smell of breakfast. She went to join her mother and told her the news.

Her mother then told *her* news. Vee, became thoughtful.

"Well, I hope it all works out well for you, mother."

"And I hope all goes well for you and Danni. God Bless you both!" she added. The two women passed just one more final day reveling in each other's company. Vee began to gather up and pack her luggage.

"Why do that? He might want to stay here with you until he gets sorted out."

"That's sweet of you mum, but you must promise you will throw us out if we become too much of a handful for you."

"Well if that should be the case I think we could probably negotiate something, rather than just throw you out."

"Ok. Thank you. I'll tell him." Before they knew it, Vee was phoning for a taxi. The two women hugged and kissed. Vee with her bag, left the house and entered the waiting taxi.

DANNI'S ARRIVAL IN THAILAND

She was in good time for the flight, which was just as well as rush-hour traffic was just starting. The driver took some detours and was soon out on the toll road. She told the driver she was meeting someone from Eva Air. They came to the Arrivals building and stopped.

"It's here," he said.

Vee paid him and went in to wait for arrivals. She had a 30 minute wait, according to the Flight Information Board. She went to a newspaper shop and picked out a magazine that might interest Danni. She found one about Music, then went to the coffee shop and looked through it while enjoying a cappuccino.

"Not as good as the Landmark," she observed. She was not at all sure whether her choice of magazine would appeal to Danni. But she was able to pass the time in comfort with something interesting. There were now 10 minutes to go. She jumped up, took her bag, placing the magazine in it, and went to the barrier. The flight had already landed and there were one or two people just coming from it. She waited and after a while more people came, many with luggage trolleys. Then, there he was, "DANNI!" she shouted. People turned to stare at her. His face lit up and he waved. He had something extra on his trolley. As soon as he came they were in each other's arms and kissing cheeks (daring enough for Thailand).

"What's this?" Vee asked.

"Thai Orchids."

"Oh beautiful!" She then told him what her mother had said and suggested he gave them to her. They found a taxi, loaded it and got in.

"Bang Na, please."

When they arrived, Madame Dee was ready, waiting for action. The driver could see exactly where to stop. His vehicle was unloaded. Danni paid him and then presented

Madame Dee with a bunch of Thai Orchids, earning himself a hug. Madame Dee went to take care of the orchids. Danni helped carry the heavier items and Vee helped too. Madame Dee showed Danni where he and Vee could put their personal things and the rooms they could use. Danni was very grateful and Vee also expressed her appreciation. Danni then said,

"As I am not paying rent, I can afford to take you two ladies out for an evening meal – any preferences?" Vee whispered to him (Landmark).

They then exited and Madame Dee locked the front door. A taxi happened to be passing and Danni waved at it. He drove to the kerb and they got in.

"Landmark, please." They soon arrived and found themselves on the pavement at the foot of the magic steps. Vee steered them towards the Chinese Restaurant. They entered and sat at their starched tablecloth with starched serviettes to examine their menus. It seemed to suggest, as Chinese Restaurants do, that what ever you choose it is going to be extremely high class and formal. There were many tempting attractions and choices were made. The same as in an Indian Restaurant, it seemed a good idea to have bowls of concoctions to share. Everyone had an enjoyable meal, including dessert and finishing with coffee.

Danni took the tab and after some time they made their way back to the foyer. Vee suddenly remembered her magazine and showed it to Danni. He thanked her and said it was very interesting. There was a general need to browse around the bookshop. It was quite late when everyone emerged and headed for the street outside. There was a row of taxis waiting so they went to the first. Not long after getting in, they were approaching the entrance to the Bang Na Housing Area. Madame Dee told the driver exactly where to stop. She unlocked her door as Danni was paying, then the 2 filed in and she closed up again. They both thanked Danni and he replied smiling, "It was my pleasure and I'm glad it was yours too." Danni and Vee said

"Good Night!" to Vee's mother, as she busied herself putting the orchids into vases. "Don't forget to spray them," Vee said.

They opened their boxes and tried to get themselves sorted. They spent about 20 minutes, then realised it could be finished in the morning. They got themselves ready in the bathroom, then came together in bed with a sheet to cover them. The air conditioner was strong and quiet. It was so good for both of them to be able to feel the other body beside them. Vee was a bit bigger now.

....

'What could be better than a fresh morning with Danni again, by my side?'

Vee found herself asking this question and she couldn't understand her uneasiness. Then Danni pulled her towards him in an embrace and she knew. The voice in her head said, "NO, I CAN'T." Danni sensed something was not quite right and released her. Vee now knew that she couldn't just switch, like a robot, from one man to another – maybe some women could, but even they didn't enjoy it. NO – Danni would have to wait for her. She owed him an explanation.

"I know this makes me sound like an old woman, but I had a very good sexual relationship with my husband, Cary. He knew me very well and I knew him very well. You are a nice man, Danni, but I have to get Cary out of my system before I can be intimate with you. I am sorry. I hope you don't mind."

"Oh, good heavens! Of course I understand. I am highly attracted to you but I haven't come here to rape you – I have come here to learn more about you, so that I can be of better value to you. So thank you for telling me honestly about your feelings. I don't want you to feel, you are under any pressure to fulfill my expectations – What I expect, is that we will both understand each other better."

"Thank you, Danni, for your understanding and

sympathy. I too want to be of better value to you. I must learn more about you, if I am to achieve that."

"Well, how about we have breakfast together?"

They both got up and began to get themselves ready, for going in search of breakfast. When quite ready, they left their room and ventured.

"Good Morning, you two!" Madame Dee said brightly as she drank her coffee. The cook brought them rice soup, then toast and marmalade and some fruit. Their coffees came last.

"It's a very comfortable suite you have provided for us."

"Well, it's the least I can do to help you out."

"We are very grateful to you, mother."

Madame Dee noticed that her daughter was not so 'over the moon' as she would expect, after a night with 'Mr. Wonderful.' Then the answer came to her. She admired her daughter for her courage and fortitude. Even with her 'problem,' she had full control. Her daughter was really amazing!

Danni's phone rang. It was his Solicitor in the UK. The money had been transferred as agreed, 50% to his UK account and 50% to his Thai account. The Royalties would go to his UK account. They would be sending a debit card to his address in Thailand. Danni gave him Madame Dee's address.

When the two women had finished speaking, Danni began.

"That was my Solicitor in the UK. We can get our own place here now and I will have to go to the bank, to get a letter for the Immigration Police."

"That's good news. Let's go and see what we can find." Madame Dee was not so enthralled to see the imminent departure of her two interesting guests. Her son, Tarrin would be back this evening, as usual, but daughters 'are different,' she mused in her sadness.

They returned to their rooms to get organized then leave the house. They started to walk and look for a taxi. Danni's phone rang again. It was Nathan.

"Hi Danni, I've retired now and with my Pension plans, I thought I would follow your advice and check out Thailand."

"It'll be great to see you."

"I will be arriving in 2 days at Suvarnabhumi (Bangkok Airport) – ok?"

"Ok give us the flight details and we'll come to meet you."

"That was Nathan, my older brother. Haven't seen him for ages! He says he's coming in 2 days. He wants to check out Thailand as somewhere to live. I said we would go to the Airport to meet him."

"Sure, no problem."

A taxi had been waiting for them.

"Sorry to keep you waiting," Danni said as they got in.

"Where to Sir?"

Vee and Danni looked at each other

"Pattaya," they both said together.

"I suggest we make the Royal Cliff Beach Hotel, our base."

VEE AND DANNI BACK

"Good suggestion."

Danni was impressed by Vee's choice of the Royal Cliff Beach Hotel. It was, it seemed to him, as comfortable and accommodating as any hotel could be. They left their luggage in their room and then ventured down to the ground floor. Vee noticed that on the TV, her programme 'Oshin' was starting. It was nearly the end of the series. She asked Danni to watch it with her. Vee suddenly realized she had watched this episode with Cary in Chennai. She said nothing about it to Danni. Oshin was now a smart middle-aged woman and her son, a grown-up young man. It showed a supermarket – the first shop of its kind in Japan. Oshin was the owner of this shop. She did not enjoy this position for very long. The programme finished with her son laying a wreath on his mother's grave. Danni said he was sorry to have missed the earlier episodes. They were both hungry.

Hand in hand they made their way to the restaurant and consulted the menu. Danni and Vee decided they would investigate the Condotel market. The same evening, after coffees, Danni checked internet for Pattaya Condotels and made a note of 3 of them, which seemed to be in the area they wanted. After unpacking and getting installed in their room, they prepared for the night – that, as they both knew, meant sleeping. Danni was careful and gentle with her (rather like Cary had been) so Vee felt, again, at ease with her man.

They woke from peaceful sleep, as a stream of sunlight found its way through a slight gap they had inadvertently left in the curtains. Danni leapt up and pulled them together. The air-conditioning was very effective. They both got themselves ready in the bathroom then dressed to go down for breakfast. Soon they were holding hands in the lift and looking at eyes. It stopped and they immediately faced front and marched out, smiling. There was a grand buffet and more than enough to eat. Their plate became laden as they walked round the display. At their table began the delightful task of eating. There was hardly time to talk.

"Yes, Condotel. Good. We will check." – was all that Danni could say, he was so busy eating. Vee said nothing. With some effort they returned to their room. More preparations and getting ready to go then – they were off!

They took a limousine and Danni gave the address of the first Condotel on his list. They came to a halt and he paid the driver.

"Thank you Sir."

"The Silver Star Hotel" was probably a 4-star, Danni thought, as they entered. A conversation with the front desk revealed that there were no condos currently available for purchase in the Silver Star.

The next Condotel was a few blocks further. As soon as they came to it, Vee realised it was the Condotel were she had stayed with Cary.

"No, please, my love, not this one. I cannot stay here." Danni was surprised, but then he remembered why Vee had reacted in such a way. He didn't comment, except to say, "Ok let's see the next one!" For this one Vee had to ask someone directions to the street on Danni's paper. After some walking they came to it. "The City Center Hotel" Their first impression was, it was smarter than the other two. Danni and Vee went to the desk. In moments, they were going up in the lift to see a Condo. Danni and Vee examined it together, going in and out of every room while looking around, trying to get the 'feel' of the place.

"What do you think?" he asked Vee.

"Let's see this one again." They entered. The two areas of interest were kitchen and bathroom.

"I think the fridge is too small, in this kitchen. The freezer is ok but a much bigger fridge is needed." They looked in the bathroom. It had good access, as it was en-suite. Vee was disappointed in the shower curtain.

"In this style of Condo you expect a sliding or folding

door." They looked at another Condo. This was not an en-suite bathroom and there was still a fridge problem in the kitchen. The next Condo seemed to be right in every way, but the air-conditioning was very noisy and not very cold.

"Well let us pray that we find something."

They went to the next floor –there was one Condo there to look at. The fridge in the kitchen was not huge, but much bigger than the others. There were 2 en-suite bathrooms. Both had showers with folding doors.

"Any faults?" Danni asked as they looked around.

"So it's this one then!"

"Yes, ok." Danni took the card and went back to the manager's office.

He negotiated a price and signed the papers that were drawn up for his bank and solicitor.

"Well after that good morning's work, I think you deserve some lunch – where shall we go?"

"Let's check 'Cary and Vees'." They took a taxi and were soon outside the restaurant. As they entered, Soosoo and Jira were on the till. Lek was rushing about with orders, helped by Noon. Prem was upstairs doing the same thing. Food was being prepared by Tan and everything seemed to be busy. There was quiet music and a hubbub of voices. The impression was that everyone was enjoying themselves. Danni and Vee found themselves a place to sit and Lek took their order. Danni had green vegetable curry and Vee had Pad Thai Vegetables. They had juice to accompany it. They then had coffees. They took their bill to Soosoo and Jira. Vee and Soosoo had a chat in Thai. Soosoo asked about her baby. She intimated that she would have a bump soon.

It was time to go. Danni and Vee said good-byes and got a taxi.

"When can we move in to the Condotel?"

"Oh, quite soon I imagine. There are official documents to be signed and bank transfers to be made. I don't think I can put a date on it yet."

"Are you getting fed up with the Royal Cliff Beach Hotel?"

"No, I am getting worried about a pain I have sometimes."

"Well, you'd better see a doctor then. I'll take you to the obst-gyn section of the hospital."

"The what?"

"Obst-gyn – it means obstetrics and gynaecology – It's just medical language for 'woman stuff.'"

"Ok but a specialist will be more expensive."

"My darling, what is your baby worth to you? Expensive is just right for you."

"Danni, you are very good to me."

They took a taxi to the Bangkok Pattaya Hospital and checked into Obst-Gyn (in Thai, of course).

"I want 'my wife' to see a specialist. She's due in 6 months but she is getting pains." Danni got Vee booked in. She disappeared with the Thai Doctor and Danni waited. After some time they both reappeared.

"Nothing to worry about," the Thai Doctor said, speaking English. But it is important for her to get a certain amount of rest. Anxiety and physical stress are both bad for her. If the pains still persist give her one of the pills I prescribe for you."

"Thank you very much, I will follow your instructions exactly," Danni replied.

They checked accounts and picked up their prescription at the pharmacy desk. "Ok my love we go back to the Hotel." Danni waved for a taxi to stop. They were soon back at the Royal Cliff beach Hotel.

"We had better make the most of our time here." Vee was neither moved nor inspired. With half-shut eyes she expressed her preference for rest. Danni took her back to their room. He ordered room-service.

"Oh they have hummus with salad. – would you like that?"

"Ok."

Danni phoned and ordered the hummus and salad x 2

with two Thai desserts and two cappuccinos. Vee looked at him.

"Thank you, my love, you are good at taking care of me."

"I hope so. But I have a life-time to learn to do it better."

There was a knock. Danni opened the door and the waiter wheeled in a trolley. Danni signed and the waiter left.

VEE AND DANNI FIND A WAY

"When you eat in your room you can wear what you like, you can be naked, if you like." In the restaurant you always have to wear those stuffy clothes.

"Ok, if that's what you want." Vee began to strip off. Danni followed suit. So they both sat at the trolley wearing minimal underclothes.

"Oh, just a minute!" Danni said leaping up and going to the door. He turned round the 'Do Not Disturb' notice and closed it again quickly. They then tried to turn their thoughts to food. There was some pitta bread for the hummus. Danni put some hummus on his stomach.

"Oh look! Can you lick it off for me?" Vee responded. Then she 'spilt' some hummus on her breast.

"Or look! Can you lick it off for me?"

Danni responded.

This orgy of body smearing and licking off went on and on, at its plodding pace, for nearly an hour, during which, they were both becoming quite excited.

The moment came, when they leapt up and transferred themselves to the bed. They were both sticky, hot and eager for action. Hugging and kissing went extremely well.

Before she knew it Vee was on top of him and gasped with pleasure as she felt him enter her. Realising she had enormous energy, Vee began moving, gyrating and working on what ever produced a result from Danni. Danni himself, was watching Vee and looking for a sign. The sign came. Vee started losing all self-control and getting wildly excited. She yelped and screamed as she jerked about and suddenly, "AAAhhr" her body tensed. Danni did his best to hold her, until finally, she relaxed and dissolved into kisses and hugs.

"Wow, you are incredible! I never thought you would do anything like that."

"I didn't think you would either. I thought you were waiting for me to write you an invitation, but it didn't work like that. You are very clever Danni."

"We had better clean up now. You shower first."

"Ok."

When Vee had finished Danni stepped into the shower. Soon they were both clean and put on clean under-clothes.

"Thai dessert, anyone?"

"Oh yes, I like this."

They ate a Thai dessert as 2 very civilized people. (Civilized people don't drink cold cappuccino.)

"By the way, there's a double advantage to this.

"Because you are happy and feel good – your baby will be happy and feel good."

"Are you sure?"

"Yes, the endorphins (feel-good hormones) in your blood – go to your baby, because it shares your blood."

"Or, I'm so pleased about that!"

They were both tired. It was sleeping time.

They were woken by a phone call. It was Danni's phone. Nathan would be arriving in 4 hours' time. Could we meet him at the airport?

"Yes, of course." The in-house phone then rang.

"Good morning Sir, there's a lady to see you – a Madame Dee."

"Excellent, send her up, please."

"You'd better get up, my sleeping beauty. Mama is coming."

"Oh my goodness!" Vee got up immediately and took herself to the bathroom. She came back to dress and Danni took her place. Then he came back to dress. There was a knock at the door, just as Danni was heaving up his trousers.

"Just a moment," he called. Vee was also trying to make herself presentable. The knock came again. Danni opened the door.

"I hope I didn't get you out of bed." Vee rushed to her mother and they embraced.

"Well, I have tried to take good care of her, but I cannot do it as well as you, Mam."

"Don't waste your time trying to flatter me. I have come to get you 2 some nourishing breakfast and see what else I can do to make myself useful."

The 3 were then ready to go down to the Sea-View Restaurant on the Hotel's ground floor.

"We cannot take too long, because my brother Nathan is arriving at Suvarnabhumi at 11am. I said we would go to meet him." Nevertheless, they enjoyed a magnificent breakfast, with a fine mixture of English and Thai goodies. Madame Dee tried muesli. She said it was quite good but wasn't enthusiastic. Vee and Danni had a little feast between them. They then had cappuccinos.

"Let me take you to the Airport," Madame Dee said.

So she ordered a limousine and the 3 got in. It swooped off with a huff.

It seemed that within minutes they were tearing along the Toll Road and seconds later turning off for the Airport.

"We are meeting someone from Eva Air."

DANNI'S BROTHER - NATHAN

"Yes Mam – I take you." Moments later they were stationary at an airport door. Danni and Vee asked the driver to wait for them. They entered the building. They were in good time. Eva Air was due to land in 20 minutes. Madame Dee had not seen Suvarnabhumi since it had been built. But it did not hold any surprises for her. The shops, boutiques, coffee bars and duty-free goods, were the same as everywhere. Danni and Vee joined her again and they went to the Eva Air arrivals barrier (where Vee had gone to meet Danni, not long ago) The plane from London Heathrow had now landed. Danni watched as people came from the plane. More people came . Then he saw Nathan. They both waved at the same time. He was tall and quite gaunt. Nathan embraced his brother, then he introduced Vee. "This is Vee's mother, Madame Dee." But as Danni was speaking Nathan's eyes were looking at Madame Dee. It seemed they needed no formal introduction. "Let's try to find our taxi. – We asked him to wait for us." They went together outside and the limousine and its driver were still there. He smiled and waved to see us. Nathan's luggage went in the boot. Then Madame Dee sat in front with the driver and Vee sat at the back with the men.

"Why don't you all come to my house now?"

"Thank you but I am afraid I have already booked the Landmark Hotel in Bangkok."

"I will go to Bangkok first, then." The driver said. The car swooped off.

"Nathan reached the Landmark and said good-bye. He looked directly at Madame Dee, and said, "See you again soon." Madame Dee's face lit up, "Yes, of course," she said automatically. They reached Bang Na shortly afterwards. Madame Dee said a polite good-bye to Danni and Vee. The 2, then returned to the Royal Cliff Beach Hotel. It was getting late, so they went to their room and got ready for bed. They slept very well.

Danni and Vee were as comfortable with each other as any couple could possibly be. They had opened their eyes, to another day. Vee was past the uncertainty she had felt with Cary. Dannie was a man whose creativity was not just in the realm of music, but also in his everyday life, especially sex – it seemed to Vee.

To Dannie, Vee was truly amazing – a woman capable of fine sexual performance despite being over 3 months into pregnancy. The performance had brought them closer together and gave them a feeling of belonging to each other.

These comfortable thoughts were suddenly interrupted by a phone ringing. It was Danni's phone.

"Good morning, how are you?"

"Just fine thank you. The Landmark is a very comfortable Hotel. I am enjoying it, but it comes at a price. I don't think I can keep this up for very long. Why don't I come and have a chat with you?"

"Yes, why not? Just come here and we'll be pleased to see you."

Then, Vee's phone rang. It was her mother. A conversation in Thai followed. It finished.

"My mother is coming here," Vee explained.

"I think she is lonely there. Tarrin comes and goes but that's no company for her. So I invited her here.

"My brother, Nathan, is coming here too - Wow, we are going to have a big group, but 'the more the merrier', is what the English say." Danni and Vee proceeded to get themselves ready and presentable to their guests. They were about to sit in armchairs when the in-house phone rang.

"A gentlemen has arrived for you, Sir."

"Thank you. Send him up please."

There was a knock at the door. Nathan entered. Danni hugged him and introduced him to Vee.

"Come in and sit down."

"Thank you. I don't know if you can help but I'm

looking for some sort of accommodation – I mean something within my budget."

There was another knock at the door. Vee stood up. Her mother entered and the 2 women hugged and kissed. Nathan's eyes followed Madame Dee as she sat down. Danni phoned room-service and ordered teas or coffees for everyone. Moments later a trolley was wheeled in and everyone was served tea or coffee. Danni signed for it and the waiter took his trolley and left.

"Well, it seems Nathan, who is new to Thailand needs some information on accommodation – Is that just Bangkok or elsewhere too?"

"I would prefer to be in Bangkok," Nathan replied. Drinks were enjoyed but Madame Dee had trouble picking hers up because her hands were shaking. Vee wondered what had come over her mother. Finally, she managed to speak,

"I, er mm want to say that I can offer accommodation to Mr Nathan," she said without looking up.

"That's very kind Mam. But I cannot accept if I don't know where you live."

"Bang Na B106," she blurted out, in a surprisingly croaky voice.

"That's a Housing Estate in the Bangkok area," Danni informed his brother.

"Thank you. I would be happy to accept."

"What? Oh, good – Yes, thank you." She said something in Thai to her daughter and Vee laughed. She realised her mother was suffering considerable embarrassment for some reason. Danni also noticed.

"Well, now we are all happy, shall we go to a place up the road for lunch?"

"Place up the road – doesn't sound very inviting."

"A local Indian Restaurant, then."

"Yes, that's better."

2 AND 2

Danni and Vee left quickly, leaving Nathan and Madame Dee to adjust to each other. They waited downstairs. Nathan and Madame Dee came, looking just like a couple who had been together all their lives. They all fitted in to a limousine and glided off towards their destination. Outside the restaurant doors, they left the limousine. Danni signed for it. "Wait here Sir?"

"No thank you. Not this time."

He drove away and they entered the open door to the 'jungle' and heard the sitar music and some squawking birds. They sat round a table and examined their menus.

Drinks arrived first. There was non-alcoholic sangria, coconut water, mango juice or pineapple juice. Everyone made a choice and was instantly served. Food selection was the next task. There were to be bowls with Tarka Dhal, Rogan Josh and Vegetable Jal Farazi. Everyone made a choice and there were fresh hot chapattis. Nathan enjoyed his new experience. The others knew what to expect, but enjoyed it no less. The desserts to follow were, Barfi, Ledou, Rasgulla, Gajjar ka Halwa, Jalebis, and Gulab Jamons.

They finished with coffees. It was a lunch to remember. 2 couples indulging themselves together.

"Well, I guess we'll want 2 taxis now,"

"What do you mean?"

"Well, this is where we 2 say good-bye to you 2, ok?"

Nathan waved at a taxi and it stopped, "Come on!" he said to Madame Dee.

Danni got his taxi. He and Vee got in.

"They did it – Nathan and your mum are together!"

"Yes, I hope they can be as happy as we are."

"Well that means if we are not happy about something, it's important to say what it is."

"True, but does that mean there is something you are

not happy about?"

"I'll tell you as soon as we get home."

The taxi pulled up at the City Center Condotel. Danni paid and they went in, took their card and shared the lift. Danni opened the door then handed Vee the card. You count to 20, then come in. He closed the door and quickly pepared himself. He was in the bedroom and down on one knee. The door was being opened. Vee came in.

"Where are you?"

"I'm in the bedroom." Vee immediately went to him.

"What are you doing?"

"Vee, my love, Will you marry me?"

"Oh Yes – Vee gasped. "Of course I will."

"Haven't we left it a bit late? asked the Knight, rising to his feet.

"I suppose so. But at least we have now made the decision."

"Let's go to find a Church."

They checked online for Churches in Bangkok.

Danni picked up 'Christ Church,' 11 Convent Road, Silom and the phone number. He called and arranged to visit at 10.30 the next morning.

Meanwhile, a new couple were arriving at Bang Na. Madame Dee, the Healer and Clairvoyant with a tall clean-shaven man, who smiled and called her 'Kom' having learned that it was her nickname. Kom opened the door and they entered.

Nathan hauled his luggage in and left it in the hall-way.

NATHAN AND KOM

She offered Nathan a cup of tea, but he refused,

"A juice will be fine," he said. She poured the same juice for herself.

"Well, what would you say to me is I were your client?"

"That is an unfair question. We both know that you are in a once-in-a-lifetime situation and I am too."

"Oh so you can talk plainly and call 'a spade, a spade.'"

"Sorry, I don't understand. I can talk plainly, yes and I hope I always tell the truth – and you?"

"Ok, I tell you honestly, I have never met anyone as fascinating and intriguing as you. You have abilities that other people only dream of."

"Yes, that is true, but don't forget I am also a human being with a – with a heart."

"So we are the same, you and me. It's just that I haven't learned to be clairvoyant and to heal others."

"Yes but you make it sound like a trade. I haven't learned how to fix plumbing but a man who has learned this can make it his trade."

"Well, what's the difference?"

"Clairvoyance is not just a set of rules and skill in applying them. It is a gift – like being able to sing well or play the piano. The ability to heal others is also like a gift. All gifts and the ability to heal, come from the Holy Spirit. It is not me who heals anyone, but the Holy Spirit, acting through me who enables me to send healing to others.

"That is amazing. I have spent my life as a doctor. I mean, a medical doctor – an MD."

"Oh really?"

"Yes, I was in Holistic Medicine. I didn't like the NHS, its rules and power structures. It seemed to me to be just trying out new products on guinea-pig patients, for the major drug companies. In my practice I often recommended diet changes and always prescribed herbs or other natural products. My patients believed in me passionately. If you don't mind my saying so, you should probably be taking spirulina, either on your breakfast cereal or sprinkled on your soup or salad."

"No, I don't take spirulina. I have never even heard of it until you told me. Don't you want to have the same gifts as me?"

"What do you think I would say if Mozart asked me that question?"

"Oh you like Mozart?"

"Most – yes."

"Classical Western Music?"

"That is what feeds my soul."

"Talking of feeding, let's go to eat. I invite you to The Landmark Hotel."

Kom's face lit up. Nathan caught her expression as if the moon had moved out from behind a cloud.

To Kom, Nathan seemed to be a real gentleman. He was not just someone ordinary but highly knowledgeable on the subject of herbs and plants used to promote health. Above all, his eyes were magnetic – the sort of eyes she had seen in books about angels and deities, that she thought, probably didn't exist among human beings – but here he was, looking straight at her. Kom was in heaven at these moments.

They reached the Landmark's magical steps. Nathan paid the driver. They ascended and went through the doors to the coffee shop. They sat and examined the menu. A waitress came.

"Good evening Sir! Good evening Mam!" she said smiling. Kom chose something Thai and Nathan had a spinach and cheese quiche.

There were also interesting cakes to choose from. Nathan chose a Danish Pastry and Kom chose a chocolate éclair. There were coffees to follow. Afterwards, at Nathan's suggestion they went to browse in the bookshop. Kom picked up a book called, 'Letters from Thailand' –

"Have you read this? I recommend it." Nathan's choice was,

"Thai Herbal Remedies." He bought his book and asked Kom about hers.

"No, I already have it."

It was time to go home. Outside they got a taxi and he took them up the road to turn round for Bang Na. In moments, they were home. Nathan paid and they entered. Kom and Nathan had become well-adjusted to each other now. Kom opened a door and said to Nathan,

"Ok, you sleep here, is that all right for you? Bathroom is there. Wardrobe is there." She said, pointing.

"Thank you." He replied, smiling at her. Kom went to her own room.

'Well, as my darling daughter would say, Thank God!' Madame Dee was excited and had great difficulty in relaxing and going to sleep. Only very slowly, tiredness overcame her.

PROBLEMS RE. WORK

In Danni's life, Dawn was just breaking. He became restless and turned over. Vee slept on despite being jostled. It was about 30 minutes later that signs of life appeared in this bedroom. They got themselves ready and Danni asked her about her 'bump.' She reported that it was ok. She could feel the baby there.

"Well, he or she, might be hungry, so we'd better get some breakfast."

They went down to the hotel restaurant, to where the breakfast buffet was lain out. No sooner had they sat down with their trays, than Danni's phone rang. It was Jira at 'Cary & Vee's.'

He reported 2 problems, his brother, Tarrrin was spending too much time chatting with Orn, instead of getting on with his job. The second problem was the name of this restaurant. Several times I have been asked,

"Can you confirm that it is still, 'Cary & Vee's?' – if so, shouldn't it be something else now?"

I confirmed this and said, it would be a matter for you, Mr. Danni, to decide."

"Ok, Jira, thanks for bringing these issues to my notice. I will call you back. Give me 1 or 2 hours."

Vee and Danni continued to enjoy their breakfast. Danni was well prepared.

"Don't forget we must call at the Church!"

He knew exactly what he was going to say to Vee's brother. But did he? Shouldn't he discuss it with Vee? When they had begun to drink their coffees he told Vee about the Orn and Tarrin problem. Vee's immediate response was that they should be spoken to and told,

"We are giving you 2, three days off, together. This is for you to sort out your personal lives together – nothing to do with us. What *is* to do with us, is that when you return, this problem does NOT return with you. You both come here to work and give all your attention to your duties."

"Thank you darling. These are words of wisdom that I will pass on to your brother."

Moments later, Danni sent Jira a text message. His reply came back,

"Thank you for your wise words and please thank Miss Vee for me too. We will do this."

He then asked Vee about the name for the restaurant.

"Isn't it time for 'Danni & Vee's?'"

FOOD-DEE

"Why not something different? It doesn't have to be our names."

"Well, what?" Danni thought for a while then said,

"Got it!"

"What is it?"

"Food-dee."

"Are you sure?"

Yes, As you know, in Thai it means 'good food' But the Brits will call it 'Foodie.'

"Well, you know English better than me."

"Does that mean you are not keen on it?"

"No, it's ok, I suppose."

"Let's see what the workers think."

He called Jira and told him the new name.

"I want to know the general opinion from everyone." Jira promised to put it to them and let him know.

"I suppose that's what you call 'a working breakfast. But the rest of the day is ours."

"Ok, so let's go to Church." They took a taxi and arrived on time at 'Christ Church in Convent Road, Silom.

The Pastor was friendly and they booked their wedding for 2 weeks' time.

"It will be with just a few friends," they told him.

They returned to their Condotel and made themselves comfortable again.

How are you feeling, my love?"

"Oh you mean me and my bump. Doing fine. He or she is starting to move more now. I'm not sure if it's a foot-baller or a ballet-dancer."

"Might be both," Danni replied. They laughed.

"But seriously you should be building up your strength these days."

"How do you know?"

"I heard some women gossiping."

"You what?"

"I have taken a serious interest in gynaecology and studied it."

"You didn't tell me that before."

"The subject didn't come up before. – Am I right then?"

"Yes, I think so. I should be building up my strength. You are quite right about that."

....

"Well let's do some relaxing. What about lying on the beach under an umbrella?"

"That sounds interesting. We'll take a couple of beach mats from the shop downstairs."

They took a taxi to Pattaya.

About 20 minutes later, Danni and Vee were lying on their mats in the shade of

a couple of umbrellas. They had bought a coconut each and the only work to be done was sucking through the straw. When Vee had finished, Danni scraped it out for her with the spoon. Then he did his own. They listened to the sea, rhythmically lapping the shore and the shouts and screeches of children.

"This is quite a famous beach, for me," Vee began.

"Oh really, why?"

"Because it's here I met my late husband's brother Rob. He had a heart attack and I found him lying on this beach just like I had seen my father lying on his back, when he had a heart attack. My father died but I knew this man could be saved from dying so I phoned the hospital for him."

"You saved his life then?"

"Yes – well that is what he told me."

"I then learned that he was really a very good man. He was very kind and generous to me. He died one day when his younger brother had come to visit. This brother's name was Cary. I learned a lot from Cary about myself and how to be a woman. Poor Cary was in a traffic accident. A few weeks later, the Policeman told me that a lorry had swerved across the road and smashed into the taxi he was travelling in. I think he said, the lorry had a puncture. I felt enormous loss when Cary died. He had been so much to me. But now there is you. How did I find you? I prayed and God gave me you, in answer to my prayers. I met you on this beach too."

"I see what you mean. It's quite a famous beach for you. But please try to relax."

"Yes Sir." Vee felt totally safe and at ease with Danni. She knew that caring for her, was his priority. With these calming pleasant thoughts, she began to doze. Danni interpreted this as a good sign. It gave him a chance to think about himself. He knew he had to buy a car as soon as possible and do all the necessary formalities, maybe Vee's mother could help. Suddenly, his phone started ringing. He quickly went away from Vee.

It was Nathan, to say that if he needed any help with Vee re. her condition, he was only a phone call away and begged him to call immediately that any problem arose, however slight. Danni thanked his brother and mentioned about his interest in acquiring a car. He called something out to Madame Dee and she replied to him.

"Vee's mother says, buy a Toyota. Go for size and comfort. Let her know when you have it – she'll help with the formalities." Danni asked him to thank her and promised to be in touch. His phone rang again. It was Jira to say that the new name for the restaurant was accepted and it would be done this morning. Danni said he would call in.

Vee opened her eyes.

"What's going on?"

"I think we should go home. I can't leave you here and I want you to rest. I have to go to the restaurant to see what they are doing with the name board."

"Ok" Vee roused herself and Danni rolled up the beach mats. They took a taxi back to the condo. They went to the bedroom and Vee got on the bed. He removed her sandals and helped her undress. Then put the sheet over her. He

217

kissed her and promised not to be long,

"Phone me, please and tell me it is okay and when you are coming."

"Yes, I promise. That's an easier promise."

"Ok." Danni left the condo, leaving 'Do not Disturb' on the door. He took a taxi to the restaurant.

He managed to enter and could see immediately that Soo-Soo and Jira were busy at the till. He checked in the kitchen and Noon was helping Prem. She stopped her work for just a moment and turned to Danni.

"Sir, I want you to know that Lek proposed to me and I accepted, so we are engaged to be married."

"Congratulations, I am delighted." Another caller arrived at the restaurant. It was the sign-writer. Danni and Jira went to explain to him what was wanted. Jira told Danni there was enough cash to pay him. Jira asked to be told about the wedding and then left, to get back to Vee. A taxi took him as soon as he stepped outside. He called Vee to say he was on his way. In just a moment he was back at the City Center Condotel. He paid the driver and went straight to his condo. He opened the door with his card and it was still and quiet. The bed was unoccupied. Vee was in the bathroom. Hearing the sound she left the bathroom and they came together to hug. It was time to rest again. This time Danni joined her.

"You know what we are going to do tomorrow?"

"No idea."

"Buy a car."

"Good – my mother will help you."

"Ok thank you. I need to be shown all the formalities."

"No problem."

A lazy day eventually came to an end and the period of serious sleep arrived.

SOO-SOO'S BIRTHDAY PARTY

The next morning brought a phone call. It was SooSoo. She and Jira were going to have a Birthday Party (for SooSoo) Danni promised to call everyone and tell them. It was decided for Sunday so that everyone was free.

"Well I have told all the couples we know."

"What about Prem? I'll ask him.

"Hi Prem! SooSoo's having a Birthday Party on Sunday. Do you have someone special you can bring?"

"Oh yes, sure I do!"

"Good check with SooSoo then, ok?"

"Sure. Thank you."

SooSoo and Jira's place was a Condotel so they hired the hotel for their party. Danni and Vee were among the first arrivals. Tan and someone he introduced as, Far, arrived next, closely followed by Tarrin and Orn. Then Prem appeared alone. He wore a slightly embarrassed smile.

"Where is she mate? What have you done with her? Come on bring her in?" Prem was unsure what to say,

"You did come with someone, didn't you?"

"Yes, I did."

"Well where is she?"

"It's not 'she' – it's 'he'"

"Oh, well, ok then."

"This is Borant," he said, introducing a smiling young man, who had none of Prem's seriousness. He put his arm round Prem and they entered the party. There was a huge spread of goodies to eat and there were numerous juices and other drinks. Suddenly, there was a call for music and the Happy Birthday tune came over the loudspeaker system. Everybody sang,

"Happy Birthday to you, Happy Birthday to you. Happy Birthday, dear SooSoo, Happy Birthday to you!" Then there followed huge applause for SooSoo. Jira was delighted that she had risen from the depths of bad reputation to the dizzy heights of popularity. His brother and Orn were obviously enjoying themselves too. Tan surprised many people, when Far explained that she had a degree from Chulalongkorn University and had worked as a pharmacist. Nathan and Kom arrived late. They each made sure to wish SooSoo a very Happy Birthday. Then SooSoo spoke to everyone,

"Well I expect you are wondering what I got for my birthday. Actually, I got the best present I could ever have, which is being with you people who are so happy and kind to me. It was Jira's idea to have a party. I am so grateful to all of you for making it so enjoyable and successful." Again there was a burst of applause.

"Hi Borant, my name's Lek, most of us all work in the same restaurant, what about you – where do you work?"

"Oh, I'm a fashion photographer. My income depends on the commissions I get." "Do you enjoy it?"

"I love it – wouldn't change my job for anything else."

"Good, I think those of us who enjoy our work are extremely lucky. How did you meet Prem?"

"There's a good internet site where gays can meet gays."

"We had no idea that Prem was gay."

"Oh yes, he's the most special one for me."

"Well I hope you both enjoy the party."

"Thanks. It's nice talking to you," Borant said, offering his hand.

Tarrin and Orn were first to leave. They were planning to get a Condotel like Jira and SooSoo.

TARRIN AND ORN - 2

As soon as they could get a day off together. They went in search of the perfect Condotel. Eventually they found the 'Classic Place Condotel' which had all the features they liked. They looked at the apartments and chose one they liked. Tarrin said he would have to go to his lawyer, pay the agreed price and sign papers before it became theirs. 3 days later, they went to move all Orn's luggage from Lat Phrao and then Tarrin brought his luggage from his mother's house. Their first night was like camping. The next morning they managed to get up early and get installed before going to work.

When Tarrin and Orn arrived home, they were both tired after working, but found a new kind of luxury. Orn was no longer in the harsh world of pain testing. But in the world of soft pink feathers and indulgence. Tarrin showed her the room-service menu. They chose a light snack each.

"Dessert?" Tarrin asked.

"I'll have a chocolate éclair."

"Ok me too," was all Orn could say. Tarrin phoned the order. Moments later there was a knock at the door. A trolley was wheeled in. Tarrin signed and gave a tip. The waiter left. Tarrin and Orn sat at the trolley to eat. They came to the chocolate éclairs. Orn watched Tarrin and copied him. They got ready for bed and were soon clean and in sweet-smelling closeness to each other. Tarrin looked into her eyes and immediately saw her suffering. She saw the eagerness in his eyes and she didn't want to disappoint him. Tarrin knew she was nowhere near ready, yet. They kissed to say, "Good night." He was glad she had all the happiness and comfort she could handle, at the moment. They both lay quietly and closed their eyes. Sleep came to them.

The shining sun woke them both and it was time for bathroom sessions and getting dressed. They were both curious to see what sort of breakfast fare the Classic Place Hotel regarded as acceptable. As soon as they were both dressed they took the lift to the ground floor. It was a buffet breakfast and seemed to be a mixture of farang and Thai. Tarrin decided on rice soup and Orn took meusli with milk. She told Tarrin it was the first time she had seen this, so she was curious to know what it tasted like.

"Good, I hope you like it. Most farangs are mad about it."

"Oh, I thought they had egg and bacon?"

"Yes, that too! You can take anything you like, to eat."

Orn looked around. There were tomatoes, beans, mushrooms. There was toast, Som-tam and some sort of noodles. There was also, melon, papaya, guava and mango. Orn had never seen such a lot of food in one place. The idea of "Eat what you want and keep doing it until you don't want any more," was quite new to her and she found it funny. After a certain time Tarrin got himself a coffee.

"Or, so you have coffee when finish eating?"

"Usually, yes, but up to you." Orn had toast and jam, then some fruit, She then got herself a coffee like Tarrin. They had been given 3 days off work to get themselves adjusted to each other. Tarrin knew exactly what this meant. Neither of them were ready for working life at the moment. They returned to the luxurious comfort of their condo. Tarrin put the 'Do not disturb' notice on the door. Then he began to strip.

"Yes, you too!" She joined in and played the game, called, 'I take off my clothes.'

The next obvious place to go, was on to the bed. Tarrin got up and went to the bathroom, to demonstrate the possibility. When he came back Orn went to the bathroom. She returned. He held her hands and looked into her eyes. There was slightly less pain. His hands moved and he held her arms. Then he moved up to her shoulders. He came closer to her and brought his face near to hers. Her hands touched his body tentatively. They went to the sides of his body and then began to hold him. She pulled him towards her body. They began to kiss. She began to feel excitement. They flopped on to the bed - Touching became fast and urgent. He touched her breast and moved in a circle around it. The other one, he did the same. They kissed again. "Or please come to me," she implored. Tarrin moved himself on top of her and removed her panties. She kicked them down her legs impatiently. He pulled them free of her. He was then ready to 'introduce' himself. Suddenly he realized she was a virgin. He positioned himself and pushed. Her face became screwed up, "Or, jep!" (it hurts!) she said, as he penetrated. He slowly managed to maintain some movement, which developed into a rhythm. Gradually she came to life and began to enjoy the rhythm. Tarrin did his best to stimulate her but he seized up and held on to her. There were kisses to show appreciation and gratitude. Tarrin was pleased with the result. It served to bring them closer together and give them a sense of belonging to each other.

"Well, congratulations, for a beginner, you did extremely well. You were fantastic!"

"Thank you. You were good too. Nobody has ever been nice to me like you. You are a very good man."

"Aren't you hungry? What about some lunch?"

"Yes, ok. I forgot about food!"

Tarrin and Orn both cleaned up in the bathroom and dressed themselves for lunch. They went down in the lift. They were soon being shown to a table. The menus, they were given, were in Thai and English.

"What is 'Toad in the hole'?"

"I don't know. Ask the waiter."

"Excuse me what is this, please?"

"Toad in the hole is sausage in batter."

"What's batter?" she asked Tarrin.

"I don't know. Why not just try it?"

"I will have steak and kidney pie, I think."

"So one steak and kidney pie and one 'toad the hole' with vegetables and gravy.

Thank you Sir. Thank you Mam."

When the food came, Orn set about hers energetically. She wasn't sure what to do with the knife but quite satisfied with the taste. Tarrin enjoyed his steak and kidney pie.

They then went for a walk together. The beach seemed to be the best place to go. They put on their flip-flops and set out. They crossed the busy road and made their way towards it. Holding hands they picked their way along the water's edge as the waves washed up again and again. Tarrin rolled up his jeans. Orn watched him and copied. They ventured into the shallow water and followed the shore-line. Orn enjoyed paddling about. Tarrin thought that perhaps it reminded her of an early childhood experience. Eventually, they came back to the beach and continued their walk with wet feet. Suddenly she grabbed Tarrin and kissed him. (this was a daring thing for a Thai girl to do).

"I love you," she said.

"I love you too," At that moment Tarrin moved in front of her, got down on one knee and said, "Will you marry me?"

Orn laughed, not at his sandy knees, but at what he had said.

"Are you quite sure it's ME you want to marry?"

"Yes, I am. Why not?"

"Because I am always a problem for you – I am a fighter!"

"I thought you had given that up."

"Yes but it's in my head and my blood."

"Any room for me there?" She laughed.

"Yes, may be."

"Ok, I will ask you again tomorrow, and then the next day and so on."

"Ok."

"Is that ok – you will marry me?"

"No – ok, you ask me again tomorrow."

DANNI - DRIVING FORCE

Next morning Danni and Vee woke with the sun and got themselves ready eagerly, being strongly aware that, just downstairs, FOOD was available. They joined the breakfast buffet and it was the usual delight. With laden plates they sat at their table. A waiter brought them drinks. Danni noticed that Vee looked relaxed and freshened, by her rest.

"I am glad you are feeling better this morning."

"How do you know? She asked with a giggle.

"Well you are eating well and I can see the brightness in your eyes."

"Thank you. You make me sound like a buffalo."

"Perhaps, but I don't know anything about them and I am pleased that you are feeling at ease."

"Yes, I am. So what are we going to do today?"

"Something we've never done before."

"Really? – now you are treating me like a child."

"Oh, sorry, old lady, we are going to buy a car."

"Good. And I am not an old lady!"

Danni leaned forward to her,

"I only said that, but it's not true. You are too beautiful to be an old lady!" Vee was amused.

"And you are too handsome to be an old man."

"I know, they keep telling me."

"Who keeps telling you?"

"I am pulling your leg."

"Pulling what?

"Your leg. It means I am having a joke at your expense."

"Oh, so nobody tells you, you are handsome."

"Not quite true. Just one person tells me – and that is enough for me."

"Who's that, your mother?"

"No, YOU!"

"Did I say that?"

"You tell me every day."

"Do I? Well I'd better tell you today. – You are too handsome to be an old man and I love you."

"Thank you. I love you too. What about the car?"

"I think we can do this with your mother's help."

"Ok I'll check with her." Vee called her mother and they spoke Thai.

"Yes, we'll go there and pick up her and Nathan, then go car-hunting. She wants to know, if you have an International Driving License."

"Yes, I have."

The result of several phone calls and follow-ups was that the decided car was a Toyota Fortuna, 2 year-old. They agreed the price but could not drive it away until insurance and plates were dealt with. Danni also needed to take his International Licence and get a Thai Driving License. Madame Dee, showed the men where they should go for these formalities. The transfer of ownership was completed and they returned to the vehicle. Danni had managed to get a Thai Driving Licence, probably because Madame Dee was with him.

Madame Dee was then able go with Danny and Nathan to an office to get insurance. Danni showed his Thai licence and passport and gave the details of his vehicle. He then said good-bye to Nathan and Madame Dee. He drove himself and Vee home.

He called Jira to pass on to him and Soo-Soo that their Wedding was coming up soon.

"Also tell Tarrin and Orn," he added.

He then drove back to the Condotel with Vee.

"That's quite enough rushing around for one day – you must be exhausted!"

"My God! How do you know?"

"I'm just very clever."

"Oh yes, I forgot." They entered the Condo and both collapsed on the bed.

Danni himself was more relaxed, to see Vee as horizontal as she could be. She turned to him. "I love you," she said with her mouth and eyes.

226

"Me too." Danni recited to the figure before him.

"Will you be ok for the wedding?"

"I think so."

"I will pray for you to be wed-able on that day."

"Thank you. Me too."

"Well, it's only 6 days now – less than a week!"

"I don't think my wedding dress will fit."

"Ok we'd better go to a woman I know, who is a dressmaker, and I'll ask her to let it out. She will measure you and know how to do it."

Danni told her the name of the shop and asked her to check with her mother.

She called. They spoke Thai. Danni waited.

"Yes, she's ok. We can go there with the dress."

"Ok we'll go tomorrow morning. Just relax now."

As days went by, it became clear to Danni that Vee was fast approaching the moment her waters would break. He called Nathan and asked him to call to give his opinion.

BUMP AND WATERS

Moments later there was a knock on his door. He looked through the peephole and saw unmistakably, his brother Nathan.

"Come in, you don't know how pleased I am to see you." They hugged and Nathan immediately looked at Vee. He took her blood pressure, assessed her body temperature and felt the bump.

"The good news is that she is in perfect health. The other news is that I think you are right. She is not going to last much longer like this. Your wedding, next Tuesday, I think, should be postponed, at least another 2 weeks – 3 - 4 weeks, better."

Danni phoned the Pastor and reported the requested date change. He understood and accepted. He then called Jira for the same purpose.

"I will call you tomorrow and in fact, every day, now, just to be sure everything is going well."

"Thank you Nathan, I appreciate your attentiveness to her."

"It's my job! I should know what to do."

"Yes, That's why I am grateful to you but the final word will be with the obst-gyn at the hospital."

"Of course. I must go now. Kom will be worried."

Vee looked at him, wondering what he meant. Then, suddenly, she knew.

Nathan left them.

"I am glad Nathan had a look at you. He has more experience than me with these things, as you might expect, being an MD."

"Yes, but my greatest need, my dear Danni, is for you, and your loving care. It is that, which means more to a woman in my situation than all the medical expertise in the world"

"Quite right my dear, after all, childbirth is not an illness. It is only because of the advance of Modern medical science, that such a fuss is made of it. Although this is true, I think you could expect more comfort than there was in poor Calpurnia's day."

"Who?"

"Calpurnia was the wife of Julius Caesar – hence Caesarean."

"Oh I see, it should be 'Calpurniarean.'"

"Absolutely!"

"But, I don't think I'll do that."

"You will be in the hands of God."

"You mean I'll be in the hands of an obst-gyn."

"You are getting very smart, Madame."

"Don't call me Madame, I'm not a strange woman to you."

"Hardly."

"What do you mean?"

"No you are absolutely NOT STRANGE you are the most familiar person in the world to me."

"Ok. Me too."

"But you are much smarter than I realised."

"Thank you."

"Let's take a look at 'Food-dee' and see how they are managing." Danni drove Vee straight there and the found a place to park. They entered and it was as if the whole restaurant came to a stand-still. Women gasped and men called out "Congratulations!' and 'Bravo!' Prem came out of the kitchen and Lek flew down the stairs. Suddenly there was tumultuous applause, from both customers and staff. Danni raised a laugh when he said, "Well. I had only a very small part to play in this. Vee then said.

"If you are thinking as I was, about his heart, well you'd be lucky if yours was as big as his. But I know you are very kind people. I wish everyone today to have 10% off their bill, Lek, can you see to that?"

There was more applause.

"Certainly, Mam." People seemed to increase their orders, so it was a brilliant marketing ploy of Vee's. Jira and Soo came to them to offer congratulations, before rushing back to the till. Tan and Noon came next to offer their thanks. The time came when Danni said,

"Thank you so much, good people but I do think Vee has been long enough on her feet and is in need of a rest. So we have to say good-bye to you."

Vee translated his words into Thai and they left. Danni drove her back to The City Center Condotel.

"That's quite enough for you," he said, as he inserted his card in the door. Vee flopped on to the bed. Danni removed her shoes and his own. He then loosened her clothing, stripped off, himself and helped her out of her clothes.

"Are you hungry? I can order room-service."

"Good idea." He showed her the menu. They both selected and then he phoned his order. They remained covered by a sheet. There was a knock at the door. The waiter came in with a trolley. He brought Danni the chit, which he signed. Danni said,

"Just a minute," as he felt in his trouser pocket and produced a tip for the waiter.

"Thank you, Sir!"

Danni put the food on their table so that they could sit and eat. He helped Vee from her bed and she went into the bathroom.

"Call me if you need help," he told her. Minutes later, Vee emerged and sat down to eat. Danni and Vee spent an enjoyable early evening together. They were both run down and the Hotel fare was exactly in answer to their needs.

They took showers and freshened themselves before returning once more to the sheets. Wearing fresh underclothes they returned to their grand resting ground. Danni knew that Vee could now do no more than sleep. Much as the great out-doors beckoned, he could simply NOT leave his Vee, especially now that she needed all the support he could give her. She lay on her back and seemed to be already sleeping. Suddenly he heard a voice.

"What are you doing?" It was Vee, speaking to him

from the land of dreams.

"I am just coming to lie beside you. I am not dreaming like you."

"Who said I was dreaming? Are you really Danni, or am I really dreaming?"

"There's only one way you can find out. Open your eyes and you'll see it's me."

Suddenly there were two very tired eyes looking at him.

"Ok you know it's me now so go to sleep peacefully."

"Yes I know it's you. Good night, my love. Thank you for taking good care of me."

"Go to sleep!"

"Ok good night, my love."

"Does your love for me never stop?"

"That's right, my love. It never sto…."

Danni himself, began to feel this infectious tiredness. They began their night together.

…………………………..

As the sun rose and blazed through the curtains, two figures slept in the now lighted room. About 2 hours passed before there were any signs of movement. They seemed to both rouse together. Vee went to the bathroom first. Danni thanked God for another beautiful day. Vee appeared half-dressed and Danni was next in the bathroom. When both ready, they left their crockery on the trolley out in the corridor and went down to breakfast. Vee just wanted fruit, she had green mango, guava, pineapple, lychee, mangosteen, rambutan, orange and limes – just a little of each. Danni had muesli with nuts and raisins. He then had toast and marmalade and finished with a coffee. Vee had mineral water. Danni was concerned about her lack of protein and carbs. Back in the room he decided to call Nathan again.

"As soon as I have got a letter from my bank and taken it with my passport to the Immigration Police, I will come over to you. – In about an hour."

231

"Ok thanks Nathan, we'll be seeing you."

They spent their time resting. Eventually there was a knock at the door. A quick check showed it to be Nathan. He entered and began the usual tests on Vee. Her blood pressure, and the feel of her 'bump.'

"I am very sure, that her waters will break, either later today, or tomorrow morning, at the latest.

"Perhaps we should take her to the hospital this afternoon, to see what the obst-gyn says about her."

"That seems to me to be a very wise idea. Think you'll be all right?"

"Yes, I think so. Ok thanks for coming, Nathan."

"Any time, old sport."

Nathan left. "I don't like him calling you 'old' – you are not 'old' so it's 'in-a-ppropriate,' I think you say."

"No he doesn't mean 'old' like an 'old man', or an 'old car', but 'old', like 'an old friend' – that's a friend who has been a friend for a long time."

"Ok thanks, I understand." Let's go then.

"Where?"

"To the Bangkok Pattaya Hospital."

They left their Condo and walked to their car. Danni drove her to the hospital and asked for the 'new baby department' He located a car park and then they walked towards the swing doors. Vee seemed slow but otherwise ok.

"Hello," he said to the desk girl. "We want to see an obst-gyn. I want his opinion about my 'wife.'"

"Just wait here Sir and Mr. Boongsarit will see you in a moment."

They sat and waited. Vee shifted and moved. Danni was unsure what was going on with her. Vee stood up and called to the desk girl

"Horng nam yu ti nai, ka?" (Excuse me, where is the toilet, please?") The girl left the desk and took her arm.

"Thank you." The desk girl returned. The door marked 'Obst-Gyn' opened.

"Mr and Mrs Harper?"

"She's just coming sir, she went to the toilet."

"No problem." Vee was brought to them.

"So your waters have *not* broken yet – is that correct?"

"Yes Sir." He then asked to feel her bump. He took her blood pressure.

"I think you'd better keep her here. I cannot understand why those waters haven't broken yet."

"Nurse, take them to Ward 7 please. I'll come along to you in a minute." The nurse took them to a waiting room. As Vee entered, it happened, her waters broke. Danni held her. Just at that moment, Mr Boongsarit, the Obst Gyn Specialist arrived.

"Or, just what I thought, but it's terribly busy here. We'll take her through and I'll let you know as soon as you can come," he said to Danni.

2 YEARS LATER

All this was 2 years ago.

Now, 'Food-Dee' has converted the property next door, so it is now twice the size. Madame Dee was again helpful with finding workers who could adapt the building to its new needs.

After the first month with both sections of 'Food-Dee' in operation, take home pay was 40% up for all employees. Lek was now the manager of the new building. His last day off was spent with his new wife, Prem's sister, Noon. Prem's kitchen has expanded, with new equipment, stove tops and ovens and access has been made from his kitchen to both buildings.

Madame Dee has found new life with Nathan and he seems, with her, to be younger than his chronological years. It seems they should have been together many years ago, at least, from when Madame Dee's husband died. Madame Dee is relieved that her daughter's life has run so smoothly and excited to be now a grandmother. To her, Nathan is one of those rare creatures, 'the ageless man.' To suggest he was a grandfather seemed ludicrous, as there was nothing aged about him. Nathan's knowledge of herbal medicine, together with Kom's healing ability, they believe, will make a formidable business machine. So, on a trial basis, they have started, 'Healing Nature,' a new herbalist and Health Food shop, on the other side of the original 'Food-Dee.' Sometimes she is a shop assistant, 'Kom.' Other times she is 'Madame Dee, the Healer'

'Food-Dee' won a Pattaya Chamber of Commerce Award – for 'Best Employer in Pattaya.' And a Second award for 'Best Thai Restaurant in Pattaya'

Noon and Lek are married. Danni and Vee were among the guests who attended their ceremony. Noon was delighted because she was pregnant (she was not 'too old,' as some women had told her).

SooSoo's daughter is now 3. They decided to call her 'Som,' after SooSoo's aunt, who was married with a farang. Jira has hinted that they may try for another soon.

Tarrin and Orn now have a Condotel. Orn accepted Tarrin's proposal and they have announced their wedding.

Tan and Far are now married and living together in their new condo.

Dannie and Vee had the wedding dress changed again, as Vee was clearly a different shape, without her bump. Their wedding was a grand occasion, attended by a huge crowd of people. It was a day off for all at 'Food-Dee' and all the staff came. Borant volunteered to do the photography for their wedding, so it appeared in 'Bangkok Post' and 'The Nation', as well as Thai newspapers and a magazine called 'Thai Society,' thanks to Borant's contacts and efforts.

They have a beautiful little daughter, Jang, who crawls about everywhere, is learning both Thai and English and mixing them up. They are thinking about another baby. Danni still has his Thai Driving License. By the end of next year, he will have his Residence Visa, which will make him, as a farang, secure in his knowledge and awareness, that Thailand is his home.

By the way, Danni *was* able to go in to the ward and he *was* with Vee when she was having her baby, as he had promised, he would be.

Lightning Source UK Ltd.
Milton Keynes UK
UKHW021138230822
407709UK00003B/383